# A History of Applied Linguistics

How has Applied Linguistics been defined and how has the field of Applied Linguistics developed over the last 30 years? Who were the leaders that pushed the agenda? What are the core publications in the field? Who are the authors that have been cited most and how is that related to leadership? What were the main themes in research? Why did formal linguistic theories lose so much ground and the interest in more socially oriented approaches grow? What has been the impact of Applied Linguistics on language teaching?

Adopting a theme-based approach, this book answers these questions and more and forms a history of Applied Linguistics from 1980. The structure of this book is largely defined by the topics covered in interviews with 40 leading international figures including Rod Ellis, Diane Larsen-Freeman, Henry Widdowson, Suresh Canagarajah and Claire Kramsch.

Supplemented with questionnaires from a further 50 key applied linguists, this is essential reading for anyone studying or researching Applied Linguistics and will be of interest to those in the related area of English Language Teaching.

**Kees de Bot** is Chair of Applied Linguistics and head of department at the University of Groningen, the Netherlands. He is the co-author of many titles including *Second Language Acquisition* (Routledge, 2005) and the co-editor of *Language Development Over the Lifespan* (Routledge, 2009).

# A History of Applied Linguistics

From 1980 to the present

## Kees de Bot

Routledge
Taylor & Francis Group

LONDON AND NEW YORK

First published 2015
by Routledge
2 Park Square, Milton Park, Abingdon, Oxon OX14 4RN

and by Routledge
711 Third Avenue, New York, NY 10017

*Routledge is an imprint of the Taylor & Francis Group, an informa business*

© 2015 Kees de Bot

*British Library Cataloguing-in-Publication Data*
A catalogue record for this book is available from the British Library

*Library of Congress Cataloging-in-Publication Data*
De Bot, Kees, author.
A history of applied linguistics : from 1980 to the present / By Kees de Bot.
pages cm
Includes index.
1. Language and languages–Study and teaching–History. 2. Applied linguistics.
P61.D44 2015
418.009–dc23
2014037939

ISBN: 978-1-138-82065-4 (hbk)
ISBN: 978-1-138-82066-1 (pbk)
ISBN: 978-1-315-74376-9 (ebk)

Typeset in Goudy
by Taylor & Francis Books

Printed in Great Britain by Ashford Colour Press Ltd.

This book is dedicated to
Theo J.M. van Els and Richard D. Lambert
who shaped my future

# Contents

# Figures

# Tables

# Preface

The idea for this book emerged in 1994. I attended the AAAL annual conference in Baltimore and after that I drove to Barnegat Light (NJ) to visit Richard D. (Dick) Lambert and his wife Sarah Moore. Dick is an emeritus professor of sociology at the University of Pennsylvania and the former director of the National Foreign Language Centre (NFLC) in Washington. There was a strong link both academically and socially between the NFLC and the Department of Applied Linguistics in Nijmegen I was part of at the time. Dick cooperated closely on language policy issues with the head of our department, Theo van Els.

I visited the NFLC regularly and had inspiring discussions on the state of foreign language education with sharp minds like Dick's, but also Dick Brecht and the late Ron Walton. After their retirement from the center I continued to visit Dick and Sarah when possible and I enjoyed Dick's clear views on the field from his perspective as a sociologist. It was during the visit in 1994 that he suggested I write a book on the sociology of AL that would contribute to the establishment of AL as a discipline. Dick always stressed the importance of the socio-political embedding of a discipline in the larger context. I am indebted to him and Theo van Els for all those years of inspiration and support. Therefore I dedicate this book to them.

Most of this book was written in the early hours of the day in Apartment 1 3775, 21st Street in San Francisco in February and March 2014. We had a sabbatical for the semester and decided to spend a few months with my wife Marjolijn's daughter Audrey, her husband Scott and their little son Benji. I am grateful for their support and for keeping me connected with the real world of a baby-dominated family, for the wine and food tours, and for the NBA games. Writing this book was a fascinating experience, but watching a 12-week-old child grow made me aware that there are more important things in life than the history of Applied Linguistics.

I am grateful for the support I got from the university library in Groningen. Peter van Laarhoven helped me discover the world of advanced biblio-metrics and Michiel Thomas provided me with the data on journal impact. Anne-Wil Harzing helped me with the analyses using her Publish or Perish program and commented on the chapter on the citation game. Hanneke Loerts helped me with some of the statistical analyses and with not informing me about what was going on in our master program during our sabbatical. Wander Lowie held the ship of Applied Linguistics while we were away, leaving us alone while no doubt many problems arose that otherwise would have needed our attention.

Louisa Semlyen, Laura Sandford and Rosemary Baron of Routledge were supportive in getting the book published in time. Anna Pot helped me very effectively with finalizing the manuscript. The anonymous reviewers of the proposal and William Grabe, Diane Larsen-Freeman, Paul Meara and Margaret Thomas gave me very useful comments and suggestions.

There would be no book without the informants that I had the pleasure to interview and those that filled out the questionnaire and provided me with additional food for thought. I particularly enjoyed the many asides that for reasons of decency never made it into the text, but that showed me that nothing that is human is foreign to even this distinguished group of scholars.

My sons Hugo and Philip advised me on this project from the very beginning in no uncertain terms and helped me to find the right focus for the text and the audience.

The Faculty of Arts of the University of Groningen made the sabbatical and therefore the book possible. I am grateful to our Dean, Professor Gerry Wakker, for her continuous support and understanding over all those years of cooperation.

My wife Marjolijn was a constant and positive-critical support by reading and commenting on chapters and helping me with the mysteries of Excel. And much more than that.

# 1  Introduction

While linguistics as a scientific discipline has a long tradition, going back to antiquity with Babylonian, Hindu and Greek traditions, Applied Linguistics (AL) is fairly young. When and where it started is a matter of debate (Kaplan 2010) and depends on the definition used. There is a long tradition of research on the history of foreign language teaching (see Kelly (1969) on 25 centuries of language teaching and Howatt (1984) on the history of English teaching), but much less on AL. It has been argued that AL resulted from the application of behaviorist principles to language teaching, resulting in the "army method" in the first half of the twentieth century in the United States. As Thomas (1998) mentions, there is a general feeling that, in particular, research on Second Language Acquisition (SLA) has a very short history. In 1988, Rutherford wrote: "Serious research in second-language acquisition has a relatively short history ... L2 acquisition study would be difficult to trace back more than perhaps fifteen years" (404). Similar remarks can be found in other introductory books on SLA. Thomas (1998) refers to this as the ahistoricity of SLA research: "Because L2 theorists consistently ignore the past as discontinuous with the present, no one tries to investigate what knowledge previous generations may have obtained about L2 learning or what questions they may have raised" (390). She shows that there are in fact connections to thinking about how second languages are learnt that go back to Augustine in the fourth century. Stern (1983) points out that there must be some relationship between teaching and some, rudimentary as it may be, theory of acquisition: "It is not clear how language instruction could take place without there existing, minimally, a rudimentary L2 acquisition theory in this sense" (119). The present book is not going to fill this gap completely, but it does present at least a description of the field at a moment in time that future historians in AL can use as a beacon. At the same time, the description does not go back much further than the time span Rutherford mentioned. The history of views on language and the relation between those views and how languages are learnt and taught is beyond the scope of this study. The aim of this book is to present the present state of the field of AL within a historical context for the decades between 1980 and 2010.

For a proper understanding of a book on the history of a field, three things are relevant. First, information about the author's background and history in the field to elucidate where in this case he comes from and what has shaped his preferences and paradigms. The second is the motivation for the time span covered and the third is a definition of the area studied.

I will briefly summarize my academic past and some publications that were pivotal in my career. My first contact with the field of AL dates from the mid 1970s, when I took a course with that title at the University of Nijmegen. In 1977, five members of staff, Theo van Els, Theo Bongaerts, AnneMieke Janssen-van Dieten, Charles van Os and Guus Extra, had published their *Handboek voor de toegepaste taalkunde: Het leren en onderwijzen van moderne vreemde talen* [*Handbook of Applied Linguistics: The Learning and Teaching of Modern Foreign Languages*]. An English version titled *Applied Linguistics and the Learning and Leaching of Foreign Languages* was published in 1984 by Edward Arnold. In their book, the authors defined AL as "the learning and teaching of foreign languages". My development was further shaped by a minor program on language psychology, offered by the Faculty of Social Sciences, and partly taught by Willem (Pim) Levelt. Part of the course was on Ulrich Neisser's book *Cognitive Psychology* (1967), which made a deep impression on me and sparked my interest in cognitive processing. During those years I taught Dutch as a second language to adult migrants with no qualification or training. After my graduation (Doktoraal, equivalent to MA) in 1977 I got a position at the phonetics department in Nijmegen, which led to my 1982 PhD thesis "Visuele feedback van intonatie" ["Visual feedback of intonation"], which reports on a number of experiments on the effectiveness of visualization of intonation contours in learning the pronunciation of a foreign language.

In 1982, I was appointed as associate professor in the departments of Dutch language and culture and applied linguistics. For the courses I taught I used Clark and Clark's *Psychology and Language: An Introduction to Psycholinguistics* (1977) and Hakuta's *Mirror of Language: The Debate on Bilingualism* (1987). I was interested in how bilinguals process words in different languages and conducted experimental work on the bilingual lexicon.

The research that I did on language attrition with colleagues like Bert Weltens and Marion Grendel was sparked by Lambert and Freed's *The Loss of Language Skills* from 1982.

In 1989, Levelt's *Speaking: From Intention to Articulation* was published. This book has been extremely important in my development. It inspired me to work on bilingual processing models, which have kept my interest until the present day.

In 1997, Diane Larsen-Freeman published her ground-breaking article on complexity theory and language learning that became the beginning of a completely new way of thinking. This marked one of the most significant paradigmatic changes in my career. Inspired by Paul van Geert, professor of developmental psychology at my university, my colleagues Wander Lowie,

Marjolijn Verspoor and I started working on the application of Dynamic Systems Theory (DST) to second language development (SLD). This led to our Routledge publication, *Second Language Acquisition: An Advanced Resource Book*, in 2005. The interest in complex adaptive systems has given direction to both our teaching and our research over the last ten years.

Over the last 25 years I have been actively involved in the development of bilingual education and Content and Language Integrated Learning (CLIL) in primary and secondary education in the Netherlands. As part of the certification team, I contributed to the development of a quality control system for bilingual schools and I have reviewed programs in many schools over all those years. Part of the review process was observing lessons, which has been a source of inspiration with respect to language learning in instructional settings.

So, over the years, I have moved from topic to topic and back. The larger part of my work was concerned with bilingual processing based on reaction time data. Moving to DST as a new perspective also meant a sometimes dramatic break with my earlier work. My "social turn" came gradually, through contacts with people working on sociocultural theory like Lantolf, Thorne and Swain, and through the increasing awareness that in a DST perspective the social and the cognitive are closely connected and essentially inseparable.

The second issue to be clarified here is the choice of the period studied, 1980 until 2010. The motivation for this is simply: this is the period I was involved in the field. Though this continues to be the case, I decided that 2010 is far enough in the past to reflect on it. The choice of the period of 1980–2010 is not inspired by important theoretical or paradigmatic shifts or the publication of pivotal books or articles, though, incidentally, it is the year in which one of the most important articles in our field, Canale and Swain's article on communicative competence, was published in *Applied Linguistics*. As the data presented in this book will show, the informants did not limit themselves to thinking about that period only. Many of the publications mentioned preceded this time window or were published after that. Still, 1980 was marked for other researchers as well. Dörnyei's autobiographical chapter: "From English language teaching to psycholinguistics: A story of three decades" (2012) also mentions the early 1980s as the beginning of his career in AL. For some it was the end of a phase: Spolsky mentioned: "1980 was a good year: that was, as you will see from my publications about the date, when I gave up on applied linguistics and argued it wasn't a useful field". Apparently he still saw some use for the label, since that same year, he, Merrill Swain and Henry Widdowson started the journal *Applied Linguistics*, which was maybe the most important event for the field in that year. The journal was to become one of the leading journals in AL.

So far I have not found anything substantial that supports my choice for 2010 as the end date. The publication of Kaplan's monumental *The Oxford Handbook of Applied Linguistics* in that year was certainly an important event.

But around that time several other handbooks of applied linguistics were published (Davies and Elder 2004; Knapp *et al.* 2007–16). All in all, the temporal demarcation will be not too strict.

The third issue concerns the definition of the field I focus on. Van Els *et al.* (1977, 1984) discuss the history of the term and point out that it probably emerged in the 1940s. Davies (2007) and Kaplan (2010) provide extensive overviews of the development of AL in different English-speaking countries and point out that, over the years, the scope of the term seems to have become wider, though learning and teaching foreign languages has continued to be a core topic. It is not my intention to solve the sometimes hotly debated issue of what constitutes AL as discussed in Chapter 3, and I don't want to exclude relevant subtopics, but at the same time it is impossible to track the development of all of these subtopics. My working definition of AL for the present book is:

The development and use of multiple languages.

"Development" encompasses acquisition and attrition, instructed and non-instructed learning, and "use" includes storage and processing, but also the societal role of multiple languages. "Multiple" refers to everything more than pure monolingualism, if that even exists, so second language, third, fourth and so on. "Languages" refers to formally distinguished languages like German and Tagalog, but also dialects, styles and registers. Since many informants commented on what AL is for them, Chapter 3 will present some of these views in more detail.

There are various ways to describe the history of an academic discipline. One can take the time line as the guiding principle, or main lines of development, or track the leading figures. This is not what I chose to do. I wanted to get the views of a large group of applied linguists who have been influential during this period. It could be argued that this is maybe more a "state of the art" than a history in the narrow sense. Nonetheless, in the chapters on trends a range of issues will be discussed that in the view of my informants changed over time.

For this project I have opted for a theme-based approach rather than a description of the development of AL over time. A time line based approach would have to describe the development of different aspects of AL research and it would easily drown in detail. Here, the state of affairs is painted in broad brushstrokes around a number of topics. The structure of this book is largely defined by the topics in the questionnaire that I used for the interviews and for the survey (see Appendix 1). In Chapter 2, I will present information about the informants for my study. Since this book is mainly built on interview data, information on how the informants were selected and contacted is crucial. Chapter 3 is about defining AL. There is a substantial body of publications on this and though these will be touched upon, the views of the interviewees and reactions to the questionnaire will be the main source. Chapter 4 discusses the leaders in our field as listed by the informants. What the main characteristics of a leader are, is not entirely clear and the question in the questionnaire was formulated fairly broadly. Chapter 5 is on the most important articles and books from this period. The informants were asked to list the 5–10 most important articles or chapters and books. The aim of this chapter was to find out to what extent there is a set of publications that the community of applied linguists consider to be crucial for the development of the field. Is there a canon of publications every applied linguist should know? Chapters 6 and 7 are probably the most historical ones, focusing on the main trends the informants noticed over the last 30 years and how these had an impact on the field. Chapter 8 deals with the dynamic turn. Chapter 9 is different from the other chapters in that it is not based on the informants' views, but on their publications. It provides data on citations and impact factors of individuals and journals. Chapter 10 reports on the question of whether AL research has led to an improvement of language learning and teaching. I realize that this issue seems to narrow the definition of AL down to language teaching, but language teaching continues to be the main field of application. Chapter 11 summarizes this book with some concluding comments. Although there will be cross-referencing between the chapters, each chapter can be read separately.

As mentioned, this book is largely based on interview data and responses to my questionnaire. In order to stick to the original phrasing as closely as possible, I used direct quotes from the spoken and written data. All quotes are marked with quotation marks (" … "). All quotes have been verified with the informant who produced it, but the context in which they are used is of course mine.

Some chapters, in particular the ones on defining AL, trends and impact on teaching, are patchworks of literal citations. I have chosen this "conceptual pointillism" in order to let individual informants' views stand out as much as possible. Their views are the dots or points that from a distance form the picture, but what the picture is, depends on the reader's perceptions. In each chapter there is a concluding paragraph that presents my picture, but these are not in-depth analyses of the views expressed. It is up to the reader to do that for herself.

One of the reviewers of this book wrote:

> One drawback of this approach is that the data is reported but not analysed and the reader is required to do almost ALL the thinking … Isn't there the slight danger that at best, this reads a little like "extracts from things my friends said about AL in their letters to me" and at worst simply read like an unfinished draft?

This may be true and the risk is there, but this is a choice I have made consciously because I feel I do not have the authority to draw final conclusions that go beyond what my informants, and indeed many of them are friends, told me.

Some of my informants will be disappointed to see the two hour interview reduced to two quotes. I have done my best to spread the number of citations over informants, but some of them simply said more or had more to say than others, or their views coincided with those of others that made listing separate names unnecessary. There were about one hundred informants in this study so I had to be selective in the use of my quotes. Also, having even more quotes would make the reading more cumbersome.

This book was not written with a specific readership in mind. It may serve researchers to connect trends and see them in their historical perspective. For students in programs on AL it may be a useful introduction with information about the origins of the field and what direction it is taking. It is not written as a course book with assignments and recommended reading, but it may well be used as such.[1]

Finally, a note on my own position in the field. This is a complex issue, since it is difficult to be objective about oneself. I could have refrained from referring to myself altogether, but informants mention my work and contributions. I have simply added the informants' comments and listings, without further additions. Whether informants have mentioned my work to please me or not, I will never know, it is not a question I asked. When I express a view that is not based on comments from my informants, I have added "in my view". Otherwise, the views mentioned are based on the surveys and interviews.

## Note

1 One of the reviewers suggested a series of seminars that requires students to read the top ten articles (see Chapter 5), discuss why they might have been chosen by the participants in this study and reflect on the relevance of the articles to their own experience of/career in AL.

## References

Canale, M. and Swain, M. (1980) "Theoretical bases of communicative approaches to second language teaching and testing", *Applied Linguistics*, vol. 1, no. 1: 1–47.

Clark, H. and Clark, E. (1977) *Psychology and Language: An Introduction to Psycholinguistics*, New York: Harcourt Brace Jovanovich.

Davies, A. (2007) *An Introduction to Applied Linguistics*, Edinburgh: Edinburgh University Press.

Davies, A. and Elder, C. (2004) *The Handbook of Applied Linguistics*, Oxford: Blackwell.

de Bot, K., Lowie, W. and Verspoor, M. (2005) *Second Language Acquisition: An Advanced Resource Book*, London: Routledge.

Dörnyei, Z. (2012) *Motivation in Language Learning*, Shanghai: Shanghai Foreign Language Education Press.

Hakuta, K. (1987) *Mirror of Language: The Debate on Bilingualism*, New York: Basic Books.

Howatt, A. (1984) *A History of English Language Teaching*, Oxford: Oxford University Press.

Kaplan, R. (ed.) (2010) *The Oxford Handbook of Applied Linguistics*, 2nd edn, Oxford: Oxford University Press.

Kelly, L. (1969) *25 Centuries of Language Teaching*, Rowley, MA: Newbury House.

Knapp, K., Antos, G. and Perrin, D. (eds) (2007–16) *Handbooks of Applied Linguistics*, Berlin: Walter de Gruyter.

Lambert, R. and Freed, B. (1982) *The Loss of Language Skills*, Rowley, MA: Newbury House.

Larsen-Freeman, D. (1997) "Chaos/complexity science and second language acquisition", *Applied Linguistics*, vol. 18, no. 2: 141–65.

Levelt, W.J.M. (1989) *Speaking: From Intention to Articulation*, Cambridge, MA: The MIT Press.

Neisser, U. (1967) *Cognitive Psychology*, New York: Appleton.

Rutherford, W. (1988) "Grammatical theory and L2 acquisition: A brief overview" in: S. Flynn and W. O'Neil (eds) *Linguistic Theory in Second Language Acquisition*, Dordrecht: Kluwer, pp. 404–16.

Stern, H. (1983) *Fundamental Concepts of Language Teaching*, Oxford: Oxford University Press.

Thomas, M. (1998) "Programmatic ahistoricity in second language acquisition theory", *Studies in Second Language Acquisition*, vol. 20, no. 3: 387–405.

van Els, T., Extra, G., van Os, C. and Bongaerts, T. (1977) *Handboek voor de Toegepaste Taalkunde: Het leren en onderwijzen van moderne vreemde talen*, Groningen: Wolters-Noordhoff.

van Els, T., Extra, G., Bongaerts, T., Janssen-van Dieten, A. and van Os, C. (1984) *Applied Linguistics and the Learning and Teaching of Foreign Languages*, London: Edward Arnold.

# 2   The informants

In this chapter the process of the data collection will be described, including the selection of informants, some of the characteristics of this group, their educational background and the role of gender, race and age. Finally, some information will be provided on how informants became affiliated with AL as their field.

## 2.1 Demarcation problems

In the next chapter I will present views on what the definition of AL is, but for the selection of the informants some decisions had to be made that followed from my own definition of AL: the development and use of multiple languages. Though this is already a broad definition, some problems with demarcation had to be solved. The first demarcation concerns the line between AL and TESOL (Teachers of English to Speakers of Other Languages). There is a group of researchers that will typically go to conferences of the American Association of Applied Linguistics (AAAL) and TESOL, some because they like to connect fundamental research with teaching practices (e.g. Diane Larsen-Freeman and Norbert Schmitt), others because they represent organizations that have contact with teachers as one of their goals (like CALPR (Centre for Advanced Language Proficiency) at Pennsylvania State University or Carla (Center for Advanced Research on Language Acquisition) at the University of Minnesota. Some names are typically connected with TESOL, such as Donald Freeman, Kathleen Bailey and Neil Anderson. All of them have played, or still play, a role in the TESOL Research Foundation (TIRF, www.tirfonline.org), which tries to support research within TESOL. They clearly belong to the two worlds of AAAL/AL and TESOL. Other people are more based in TESOL, like Marianne Celce-Murcia and David Nunan, though they certainly have done work that would qualify as AL.

The general feeling among the informants is that TESOL is aimed primarily at teaching, teachers and teaching materials, while AAAL is more focused on research, though this will often be research on teaching and learning. Also, TESOL is about English, as its name suggests, while AAAL aims at a larger range of languages, though as will become evident later English is also dominant in AAAL.

A second demarcation problem exists with the large group of researchers doing experimental work on multilingual processing, such as Albert Costa, Ton Dijkstra, Annette de Groot, Janet van Hell and Judith Kroll. Though their work has been influential, and some of it is core AL, they have not been included in the list because they would not define themselves primarily as applied linguists. Since the work of this large group of researchers is primarily based in psychology, they would not be able to contribute to this study when it comes to bringing in a historical perspective. In addition, co-citation data gathered by Paul Meara (2012, 2014, to be discussed in more detail in Chapter 9) show that, at least for research on vocabulary, the psycholinguists form a cluster that is clearly separated from the mainstream AL vocabulary group.

The third demarcation problem is with the researchers doing neuro-linguistic research, which includes both work on language pathology (bilingual aphasia, bilingual aspects of neuro-degeneration, including aging) and work on neuro-imaging. Again, this is a world of its own, and certainly there are researchers like Lorraine Obler and Michel Paradis who have been influential, but whose work is not essentially AL.

I realize that these demarcations are arbitrary to a certain point and that it would be easier if researchers in these traditions would state that they do not consider themselves as applied linguists (as Marianne Celce-Murcia did), rather than me saying this more or less arbitrarily. Other demarcations are easier because the definition used is clear in at least one respect: the research has to do with more than one language. This means that first language acquisition, conversational analysis, discourse analysis, forensic linguistics, text linguistics and stylistics, to name just a few topics, will not be discussed here unless the research includes more than one language.

## 2.2 Representativeness

Research like this should be based on a survey of the population that covers all the various subgroups and communities. The sample should in that sense be representative of the population. As some of the informants pointed out, that is not the case here. Like the definition of what constitutes AL, the selection of informants was based on my own network and knowledge of the field. This means that it tends to be western Europe and North America biased and to overlap to a considerable extent with the people attending the AAAL annual conferences. I asked all my informants to give me names of people I should contact and that certainly helped to make the sample more representative. Nevertheless, as the lists of informants interviewed and surveyed in Tables 2.1 and 2.2 show, the bias is still there. The overwhelming majority is from the United States, there is a sizable number of British and Canadian informants, but small numbers from other countries like Sweden,

*Table 2.1* List of interviewees

| | |
|---|---|
| Lyle Bachman | Keiko Koda |
| Camilla Bardel | Claire Kramsch |
| Heidi Byrnes | Richard Lambert |
| Suresh Canagarajah | James Lantolf |
| Chris Candlin | Diane Larsen-Freeman |
| Andrew Cohen | Tim McNamara |
| Vivian Cook | Sinfree Makoni |
| Jodi Crandall | Lourdes Ortega |
| Robert DeKeyser | Norbert Schmitt |
| Rod Ellis | John Schumann |
| Theo van Els | Elana Shohamy |
| Suzanne Flynn | Barbara Seidlhofer |
| Susan Gass | David Singleton |
| William Grabe | Merrill Swain |
| Karen Johnson | Elaine Tarone |
| Alan Juffs | Margaret Thomas |
| Gabrielle Kasper | Richard Tucker |
| Eric Kellerman | Andrea Tyler |
| Joan Kelly Hall | Henry Widdowson |
| Celeste Kinginger | Terrence Wiley |

PRC, Denmark, Finland, Germany, Israel, the Netherlands, Austria, Australia, New Zealand, South Africa and Spain. There are no informants from South/ Middle America and the southern and eastern part of Europe, apart from Spain.

This does not mean that there is no relevant research being done in the countries that have not been included, but during the period covered no centers of gravity in these regions have played a major role, maybe with the exception of Singapore. Looking at the presentations at the annual AAAL conference and related conferences, there is an enormous volume of work by researchers from countries like Japan, Korea and China, but most of that work results from graduate training in western universities, since few of them give a university outside the United States/Canada/Australia as their affiliation. No doubt this will have an impact on the field in the long run, but it is not yet really visible in the period covered here. Writing a history of AL in Asia would make a fascinating study, but it is not the one reported on here.

Representativeness may therefore be a problem, but is it really? There is no doubt a lot of relevant research being carried out all over the world. But not all of that is accessible, which means published in English-language media. As Andrew Cohen noticed, there is a very active AL community with several journals in Brazil, but all of that is published in Portuguese, which very few applied linguists in other countries will be able to read. I know that there is excellent research on AL in Germany because I happen to be able to read German, but the fact is that I do not read German articles and books on a regular basis. Furthermore, as far as researchers from German-speaking

*Table 2.2* List of informants invited to fill out the questionnaire

| | |
|---|---|
| Charles Alderson | Joseph Lo Bianco |
| Neil Anderson | Michael Long |
| Paul Angelis | Anna Mauranen |
| Kathi Bailey | Mary McGroarty |
| Kathleen Bardovi-Harlig | Paul Meara |
| Margie Berns | Rosamond Mitchell |
| Anne Burns | Carmen Muñoz |
| Martin Bygate | Paul Nation |
| Jasone Cenoz | Howard Nicholas |
| Carol Chapelle | John Norris |
| Harald Clahsen | Rebecca Oxford |
| Guy Cook | Aneta Pavlenko |
| David Crystal | Alastair Pennycook |
| Alister Cumming | Manfred Pienemann |
| Jim Cummins | María del Pilar García Mayo |
| Alan Davies | Ben Rampton |
| Annick De Houwer | Tom Ricento |
| Jean-Marc Dewaele | Peter Robinson |
| Zoltán Dörnyei | Bernd Rüschoff |
| Patsy Duff | Dick Schmidt |
| Hannele Dufva | Bonnie Schwartz |
| Nick Ellis | Michael Sharwood Smith |
| Donald Freeman | Roger Shuy |
| Durk Gorter | Tove Skutnabb-Kangas |
| Kevin Gregg | Antonella Sorace |
| Marianne Gullberg | Nina Spada |
| Roger Hawkins | Bernard Spolsky |
| Jan Hulstijn | Bill VanPatten |
| Kenneth Hyltenstam | Johannes Wagner |
| Keith Johnson | Wang Chuming |
| Wolfgang Klein | Albert Weideman |
| Karlfried Knapp | Lydia White |
| Elizabeth Lanza | Ruiying Yang |
| Patsy Lightbown | Richard Young |

countries have had an impact it is through the same books, journals and conferences as the English-speaking researchers use and attend.

For a survey like the present one, there are various ways to sample informants. Ideally, the total population is defined as precisely as possible. Then, a sample could be drawn using parameters such as nationality, training, current research interests, knowledge of the field and so on. However, there is no exhaustive list of applied linguists around the world, nor an exhaustive list of research topics, and that makes the sampling problematic. I could also have asked all the affiliates of the Association Internationale de Linguistique Appliquée (AILA) to distribute my questionnaire among its members, but that might have led to an unmanageable number of responses. Also, the response might have been very low. By using my contacts in the AL world I hoped to get a high response of people that matter. Of course, all applied linguists are equal, but some are more equal than others. In the end, the selection of informants was done on the basis of my intuition and my knowledge of the field, overviews in journals and handbooks, and attendance of conferences. And, as mentioned earlier, I asked all informants I interviewed to give me names of people to include. This led to a first list of informants I could interview at different occasions; during conferences, but also during visits.

In early 2014 a sabbatical allowed me to interview several people on the East Coast and in the Bay area of the United States. Ideally, I would have interviewed all the people on my (constantly growing) list, but it became clear that the resources in terms of money and time were too limited. I managed to complete 38 face-to-face interviews in the end, and sent out the questionnaire to fill out to 68 additional informants. Table 2.1 lists the informants interviewed and Table 2.2 lists the informants contacted for the questionnaire.

The questionnaire was returned, after several reminders, by 56 informants. The data collection was ended on May 1, 2014. Some people indicated that they did not feel that they were applied linguists, like Harald Clahsen, who now sees himself more as a psycholinguist. The informants were contacted by e-mail, and there is no guarantee that those who did not respond actually received the e-mail. Therefore, non-response will not be reported on with names. To what extent the non-response has led to a bias is unclear.

## 2.3 Gender aspects

In the interview, Elana Shohamy stated: "Men stick with men." I never felt like I was that kind of man, but here was an opportunity to test to what extent this statement was true for the group of informants in my study. When I selected the informants, gender was not on my mind. That in itself already suggests a bias, but the data in the survey allowed me to go further: who did my informants see as leaders in the field and who were they influenced by. In the list of informants, there are 45 women and 61 men. In the questionnaire there was an item on who else I should contact, and in most cases I followed that up. I did not try to compensate for a gender imbalance. But I now realize that by emphasizing the impact of citations and h-indices, there is a bias, since that kind of competition is typically seen as a male rather than a female characteristic. There may be women who have been very important in the field, but never aimed at publishing internationally. When the informants do not mention them, such individuals are very difficult to spot. One example from my own past is that my thinking about AL and testing has certainly been influenced by my former colleague AnneMieke Janssen-van Dieten in Nijmegen, who was very active in the Dutch testing scene, in particular with respect to teaching and testing of Dutch as a second language. It might have been better to specifically ask which women have influenced my informants.

The primary selection, of course, had an impact on other data, such as who are seen as the leaders and who wrote the most important articles and

*Table 2.3* Gender effects in listing leaders in the field

|                    | Male leaders | Female leaders |
| ------------------ | ------------ | -------------- |
| Male informants    | 575          | 291            |
| Female informants  | 345          | 230            |
| Total              | 920          | 521            |

books. For this, it was tallied how often male/female respondents listed males/females. Table 2.3 presents the number of male and female leaders mentioned by male and female informants.

Both men and women mention more men than women as leaders. This is confirmed by a Chi-square test (ChiSq (2). = 10.26, p < .001). So for the mentioning of leaders, the gender bias is clearly there: male informants mention male leaders relatively more often than female leaders, though female informants also mention men relatively more often as leaders than women. The data seem to show that Elana Shohamy is right in the sense that men tend to list more men as leaders than women, but women also mention more men. So yes, men stick with men but so do women.

Heidi Byrnes sees another difference between men and women: "Women are less attached to one paradigm and more willing to change and seek new ways. They tend to be more issue-driven than theory-driven." Since there was not a specific question on this and the issue emerged too late to include it in the interviews, my data do not provide answers on this issue.

## 2.4 Race

AL is largely a white enterprise with more recently a growth of the number of researchers from Asia. Many of them do doctoral work at English-speaking universities, though there are centers like Singapore, Hong Kong, Guanzhou and Xi'an in China where significant work in AL is being done. As mentioned earlier, the coverage of areas outside the English-speaking world and western Europe is very limited. The lack of representation from these regions may be a reflection of the problems researchers in those areas have to get their articles and books published and their grant applications accepted: problems concerning a lack of knowledge of academic English, but also the highly restrictive definition of academic English by journal reviewers and editors. In general, race is a complex issue that is rarely addressed in AL research, it seems. There is a remarkable lack of Afro-Americans working in this field. Finding out why that is, would be another study.

## 2.5 Age

No information was asked about the informants' age, but many mentioned the year of their graduating which provides some clues about age (and at least one refused to tell the date of his graduation because that might provide clues about his age). In my selection of informants I tried to include people who have been active in the field for most of the period of 1980–2010, so some people have not been invited to participate because they were too young. Informants who defended their PhD after 2000 were not included, though some exceptions were made for colleagues whom I thought would have in-depth knowledge of what has happened in the past even though they may not have "lived" it. Lourdes Ortega and Marianne Gullberg are obvious examples. The estimated range of ages is between 40 and 75 with a large proportion in the 55–65 range. The effect of age may be different in different countries. In the Netherlands, there is mandatory retirement at age 65. Though some universities will have facilities for emeriti, there is typically no support for conference attendance or costs for data collection, which makes active participation in the field more cumbersome. In other countries, there is no mandatory retirement, though many universities have incentives for elderly professors to take part-time retirement. So for this group of informants there may be differences in level of activity depending on the retirement conditions.

## 2.6 Multilingual applied linguists?

One of the questions in the questionnaire was whether the informants read AL literature in other languages than English. The answer is basically: "No, I don't (unfortunately)." There is quite some shame about this, in particular among the applied linguists from English-speaking countries, who confess not to have any knowledge of other languages. But apart from a small number of really international researchers, such as Heidi Byrnes, James Lantolf and Claire Kramsch, to name just a few, even those informants who are multilingual and should be able to read literature in other languages indicate that in fact they do not. There are various reasons for this. One is that there is already so much literature in English that it is hard to even keep up with that. The other reason is that the national communities of AL are also different discourse communities with their own ways of expressing things. Even for core concepts, like "learning", "teaching" and "multiculturalism", there are marked differences between these discourse communities, which makes cross-referencing problematic. This does not necessarily mean that a whole national AL community is disconnected from the mainstream as shown by the internationally very active AL community in Spain. It is not clear why the Italian and French communities are so much separated from the international AL community, while Spain is so active and connected. It is quite likely that leading researchers such as Rosa Manchón, Carmen Muñoz, María del Pilar García Mayo and Jasone Cenoz play an important role in this.

The strong tendency to rely on English only has in some respects negative effects. Camilla Bardel mentioned that in the foreign language departments in Sweden the main thesis still has to be written in the foreign language (Italian,

French), but that younger researchers increasingly protest against this practice since that impedes their work from becoming known internationally. Finally, the power of English when it comes to publishing is such that most researchers will publish their best work in English-language media. So, as Robert DeKeyser noticed, to a certain extent the publications written in another language seldom represent an individual researcher's best work. This may lead to a gap between researchers and practitioners.

## 2.7 Educational background

Educational systems differ between countries, but in most systems there are three steps in academic education: BA, MA and PhD. In the British system, there are also diplomas, honors degrees and there is not necessarily an MA when there is a PhD. I will report on where the informants' MA and PhD degrees were awarded. The question behind the analysis of the educational backgrounds is whether there are, or were, specific centers or programs that produced significant numbers of applied linguists who have shaped the field.

The 106 informants have been educated in 64 different institutions for their MA. Four universities have been mentioned four times: Essex, London (UCL and Institute of Education), Reading and the University of Southern California. For the PhD, 63 different universities are mentioned. UCLA is mentioned five times, London and Georgetown four times and McGill three times. As far as countries are concerned, five informants mention a German institute, three a Dutch institute, two a Danish institute, two a Belgian institute and two a Spanish institute. One institute is mentioned for Australia, China, Finland, France, Hungary, Italy, Poland, New Zealand, Poland and Sweden.

There is an interesting switch toward North American universities from MA to PhD: while for the MA, 25 informants mention a UK-based institution, the number goes down to 14 for the PhD, which reflects the move to the United States mentioned by many British informants. At the same time, the Edinburgh program set up by Pit Corder is mentioned frequently also by American informants who spent some time there, but apparently few informants actually completed their degree there.

For the US situation, Thomas (2013) describes the institutional history of PhD programs, addressing only those which specifically offer doctoral degrees in "Second Language Acquisition" or "Second Language Studies". The point was to study the emergence of graduate programs that adopted those names, as symbolic of the rising sense of independence in the field. Thomas focuses on nine existing programs in order of their foundation:

- University of Hawaii at Manoa (1989)
- University of Arizona (1991)
- Carnegie Mellon University (1995)
- University of South Florida (1999)

- University of Iowa (2000)
- University of Wisconsin at Madison (2002)
- Indiana University (2002)
- Michigan State University (2004)
- University of Maryland at College Park (2008).

Programs outside the United States were not included, for lack of awarding a degree with the name "SLA/SLS". Thomas writes: "The focus here is on the institutionalization of the PhD in SLA. Due to the convergence of whatever historical, political, intellectual and institutional factors, to the best of my knowledge that has so far taken place in the United States" (Thomas 2013: 513).

It is no doubt true that US-style PhD programs are mainly found in the United States, but similar programs exist in other countries. In the Netherlands, PhD programs are generally labeled more broadly, like "linguistics", but the PhD awarded is a university one, not one from the Faculty of Arts or Social Sciences, so using the criteria Thomas applied, no such degrees are awarded in the Dutch system. Also, the programs listed focus on SLA/SLS, which does not coincide with programs in AL. "Certainly the long-contested definition of 'applied linguistics' (Davies and Elder, 2004) is not equivalent to the definition of 'SLA', so that labeling a degree or program with one of these terms over the other carries weight" (Thomas 2013, 513–14). For the purposes of this book, the overlap between the two terms warrant the reference to these programs, since these are likely to educate the next generation of SLA/AL researchers. The fact that the oldest program started only in 1989 shows that the institutionalization of such programs is of recent date. The fact that so many programs (and many more related ones) exist and appear to attract significant numbers of students is a sign of the firm position of AL in many university settings. As several of the informants indicated, the time that AL was secondary to theoretical linguistics and literary studies seems to have passed, which may have to do with the demise of the Universal Grammar (UG) school and the growing awareness of the applicability of AL research to real world problems.

The list of nine SLA programs contains only a few of the universities that our informants received their degree from: Illinois at Urbana-Champaign, UCLA and Stanford. A quick internet search using "PhD programs in applied linguistics" as the main search term leads to a list of programs, including Pennsylvania State University, Iowa State, Columbia, Georgetown, Memphis, San Francisco State, Northern Arizona State and the University of Massachusetts to list some of the US-based ones, but also in other countries, like Carlton (Canada), Lancaster (UK), Münster (Germany) and Groningen (the Netherlands).

Over the last decades many programs in AL, either independent or as part of linguistic programs, have been set up, not only in the United States but also elsewhere. It can be concluded that over these decades, programs in AL have established themselves with a growing tendency to break away from the linguistic programs they were traditionally part of. As some of the informants mentioned: "Is it really useful for an AL student to take courses on historical phonology?" At the same time, several informants, including Antonella Sorace, Kathleen Bardovi-Harlig and Martin Bygate, deplore the decline of the linguistics content in degrees in AL or SLS. The fight over what should be in an AL program continues at many universities. In a way, programs leading to a degree in SLA/SLS have an easier time positioning themselves vis-à-vis traditional linguistic programs, since they are not confronted with the all too familiar argument that for an applied linguist, someone who applies linguistics, a firm basis in theoretical linguistics is mandatory. This is one of the issues that relate to the sociology of a discipline: due to an array of reasons, there is reportedly an increase in students interested in AL and a declining number of students opting for theoretical linguistics. Student numbers are relevant for jobs and positions, both existing and new ones. Fortunately, student numbers, in particular majors, are not always and everywhere the only criterion for the sustainability of language programs. Heidi Byrnes points out that at Georgetown the number of students that come from other disciplines who take a language course and stay on to take more courses is seen as a more important criterion, since it shows that languages are relevant also beyond the humanities.

## 2.8 Affiliation with AL

This question generated a list of personal stories of how the informants got involved in AL. When asked how he got involved in AL, Guy Cook replied:

> By accident. In 1983, I returned from 3 years teaching English in Moscow. I had no job, no house, no money, and a young Soviet bride. Taking pity on me, Terry Sandell at the British Council in Moscow offered me a full British Council grant to study an MA. I was offered places at Edinburgh and London. I chose London. I was so enthralled and inspired by the teaching of Henry Widdowson and Chris Brumfit, that I became an AL.

Ben Rampton's story was somewhat different:

> I started out as a state school ESOL teacher, working in a language center for children who had recently arrived in the UK. One year, children stopped arriving, so the Head of the centre went round local schools picking out children who were having difficulties with reading and had brown faces. This generated a class that I then had to teach with ESOL methodologies – it was completely inappropriate as all these kids were fluent speakers of English and just needed some help with literacy. I realized that there were problems with the educational and linguistic

ideologies that justified my Head of centre's strategy, and so I did an MA to try and figure out more clearly what the problems were, and how the ideologies could be changed.

Since there were few programs specifically on AL, many of my informants came to AL via teaching English as a foreign language, often without any qualification other than being a native speaker. For instance Richard Young:

> After I came down from Oxford with a degree in Philosophy, Politics and Economics, the first job I found was as a teacher of EFL in Italy, where I taught in private language schools and at the University of Torino. Toward the end of my stay in Italy, I became curious about the social dynamics driving language teaching, learning, and applied linguistics.

His case is typical for how many people found out about AL, first a teaching experience abroad and an ensuing interest in theoretical aspects of language learning and teaching.

Not all informants started out teaching English. Donald Freeman taught French in secondary education, and "I found the work fascinating, and by the end of that year I'd decided I wanted to learn more about language teaching, which led me to the School for International Training, where I did my MA". Jim Lantolf taught Spanish in secondary schools and found it frustrating and not very rewarding. Alan Juffs taught English in secondary education, and liked it. Johannes Wagner taught German as a foreign language to Japanese students, and I myself taught Dutch to Turkish immigrants. Some informants got interested in language teaching at an early age: Annick De Houwer: "I started out as a language teacher (teaching English and Dutch) – private, paid lessons – to peers and a six to nine-year-old neighbor boy when I was a teenager."

Many applied linguists entered the field through teaching a foreign language and realizing that they missed the theories behind it and that they would be better teachers if they could gain a better understanding of what learning another language entails. Thomas Ricento's story is typical:

> I was an ESL instructor, then director of a program that taught ESL to mostly welfare recipients in Boston in the early 1970s. Later, when I was teaching ESL in Southern California, I decided to enroll at USC to get a better grounding in teaching. I studied mostly theoretical linguistics at USC and found that I was more interested in studying real language in real use, and especially the social and political aspects.

Other people, like David Singleton, wanted to do something useful: "I thought doing linguistics might be useful, which, it turned out, wasn't the case in Cambridge in the 1970s."

At least two informants, Zoltán Dörnyei and Lourdes Ortega, indicated that they became applied linguists out of frustration with their teaching experience. As Dörnyei writes in his 2012 autobiographical chapter: "I was very much a language teacher at heart, but a *frustrated* language teacher. I was aware of the almost unlimited possibilities within language teaching ... but I was far less successful in trying to figure out why certain things worked better than others" (2012: 3). Along similar lines Lourdes Ortega mentioned that she had done all the teacher training courses she could find, but felt that the research on language learning and teaching did not trickle down from research through teacher trainers to learners. "Researchers do not make content relevant for teachers. My job is to make research relevant."

Other informants wanted to enhance their expertise because they were confronted with specific problems in their teaching. Ruiying Yang remembers: "I became interested in a course on genre analysis because it could help me solve the problems that Chinese EFL learners had when reading and writing research papers." Mary McGroarty reports similar experiences:

> Among those I tutored were several native speakers of Spanish; for some (not all), Spanish transfer issues were evident. I also came to see that, for some of these students, having a different language background was not a major issue, but lack of familiarity with academic skills surrounding literacy expectations at university level was.

A similar problem pertaining to motivation played a role in Karlfried Knapp's career:

> At the time I completed my MA, I became aware of the language problems of migrant workers in Germany. I began to work as a volunteer in a community center teaching migrant workers German as a foreign language and helping them in their dealings with public authorities. I soon realized, however, that traditional approaches to foreign language teaching were inadequate for this clientele, and that in addition to insufficient command of German, the migrants also encountered severe problems on the level of culture in interactions with Germans, in particular in the context of official organizations and institutions.

There seems to be a tendency for researchers who started out teaching English abroad without learning a local language to stick to EFL/ESL in their later research, while researchers like Patricia Duff, but also Diane Larsen-Freeman and Andrew Cohen, broadened their research to other languages than English. According to Margaret Thomas, this background and experience in ESL still defines the research focus: "Given that so many applied linguists entered the field through teaching ESL at universities, it is not surprising that the focus is still on the same target group and focused on English." This echoes Lourdes Ortega's observation that most of the research focuses on adults or adolescents who are well off. There is research on minorities and heritage speakers, but that focuses more on language policy issues than the process of learning. Also, the attention to K-12 has traditionally been limited in the North American AL community, while in Canada there is substantial research by Fred Genesee, Merrill Swain and others on various forms of immersion.

In some cases international developments impacted on people's involvement with language teaching and AL. Zoltán Dörnyei mentioned that the fall of the Berlin Wall in 1989 and the need for English language teaching that emerged as an indirect result of that, defined his career: "Thanks to this fortunate coincidence of language globalization and favorable market conditions, even undergraduate English majors such as myself were offered lucrative teaching contracts that few of us could resist."

Another route to AL was through research. Rebecca Oxford worked as a consultant when she was asked to do research on language learning strategies. Paul Angelis became involved through his work as a Canadian representative to AILA and presenting at the AILA Congress in Copenhagen in 1972. He then went on to contribute to the foundation of AAAL. Similarly, Hannele Dufva got interested in AL through research on L2 phonetics and the establishment of the Finnish Association of Applied Linguistics (AFinLA).

Though their perspectives on testing may have changed over time Lyle Bachman and Tim McNamara both became testers by being thrown in at the deep end, with no real preparation. Lyle Bachman recalls:

> What I was expected to do was develop and administer a placement test for the intensive English program at the national language center in Bangkok. I knew nothing about this. There were two references in the library: Robert Lado's seminal *Language Testing* (1961), and John Carroll's *Fundamental Considerations in Testing for English Language Proficiency of Foreign Students* (1961).

Tim McNamara had two weeks to read himself into testing, listening to lectures he got from other students on his Walkman while cooking dinner.

For most people becoming an AL was a gradual process, but there are examples of a more sudden change. Margaret Thomas remembers vividly when she decided to move from theoretical linguistics to the history of AL:

> It was at AAAL 1991 in NYC, and I was attending a presentation by a well known researcher who gave a very studious overview of the research on the accessibility of UG after puberty. I had just finished my dissertation and knew this stuff in and out. The room was in some high building with a low ceiling. The room was full and claustrophobic, it was too warm, I was ten weeks pregnant and very nauseous. Jackie Schachter sat down in the row directly in front of me. She draped a beautiful

pastel cashmere sweater on the back of her chair, almost falling into my lap. Suddenly, I felt like throwing up. I felt that my academic future was completely locked in this tiny space, the room was too full, the ceiling too low and I was about to throw up over Jackie Schachter's beautiful sweater! I felt physically and intellectually trapped and tried to think of something new in order to make it to the end of the talk. What did people in other places and times think about learning languages? Could we look at SLA in some other time frame? It happened then to me, a totally different interest. I didn't know anything about the history of language teaching, but decided there and then that this was my future.

Other people got into the field on the basis of their personal interest. Tove Skutnabb-Kangas recalls:

I got involved in bilingualism and bilingual education partly because of my own bilingualism from birth (two mother tongues, Finnish and Swedish), something that I always thought of as very positive. My mother started teaching me Latin when I was four, and the experiences that it gave me of metalinguistic awareness made me very interested in languages.

## 2.9 Influenced by ...

The item in the questionnaire was: "Who were you influenced by?" Responses showed considerable overlap with the names mentioned under "leaders", to be discussed in Chapter 4. Occasionally informants mentioned people who were important for them even though on an international scale these people were not seen as leaders. An example is Terry Quinn from Melbourne, whom Tim McNamara mentioned as having played an important role to him. Though Quinn is not generally seen as a leader in the field internationally, he clearly influenced several people in the Australian context.

The aim of this question was to see whether there are lineages or core persons who were central in the field by having influenced a significant number of informants. Mentors and supervisors are typically mentioned, but quite often also researchers from fields outside of AL. The data on "influenced by" show the degree to which AL is a discipline that borders on many other disciplines and that is inspired by developments in adjacent fields. Names like Goffman, Cicourel, Heritage, Bourdieu, Foucault and Schlegoff are mentioned regularly, while they certainly would not define themselves as applied linguists or as leading the field of AL.

Another complicating factor was that some people provided a whole list of names, and others just a few. Andrew Cohen generously mentioned 15 people, Tove Skutnabb-Kangas some 87, while Paul Nation says: "This is not a field of leaders" and he mentions three. So any counts of who were influential would be biased, unless the listings are weighed. Because many informants did not distinguish between "leaders" and "influenced by", and there were such enormous differences between those who mentioned many influences while others mentioned just a few, the data on "influenced by" are not analyzed further.

## 2.10 Influence on ...

The aim of this question was to see to what extent there are connections in time between generations. While the "influenced by" reflects the past, the "influence on" should provide a picture of who will be the next generation. Few people were able or willing to state that they had a clear influence on other people, apart from "my students". Some informants, when prompted, mentioned names of students who have become influential in the field. Merrill Swain, for instance, said that she assumed she had had some influence on her students. She also suggested that she had influenced many Canadian parents and educators with respect to French immersion programs. Some informants were less than reluctant to claim their impact, but many refrained from mentioning names, and referred to the graduate students they had supervised and what positions these had gained in academia, e.g. Lydia White who mentioned her students Alan Juffs, Silvina Montrul and Roumyana Slabakova, who all have been very successful academically. Merrill Swain mentioned Roy Lyster along with a number of other students, Theo van Els mentioned Nanna Poulissen and myself. While we typically think of succeeding generations when it comes to "influence on" or "influenced by", there are also cases where graduate students are mentioned as an influence, like Gisela Granena mentioned by Michael Long. In most cases the influence was seen as mutual as mentioned by Andrea Tyler with respect to Nick Ellis.

A database was set up to list all contacts. The databases used did not allow me to check whether the "influence on" information was matched by the "influenced by" information: when X mentioned having influenced Y, it was not always the case that Y mentioned being influenced by X, but this was not checked systematically. A mismatch might actually be embarrassing.

"Influence on" appeared to have many forms. It can be based on an exchange of ideas or books read, but also on contributions to a person's career, through alerting people to positions available or recommendations for applications. A good example of this is Dick Tucker. A general Google search reveals that many people express their gratitude to him because of his support in their applications/projects/careers.

Some people are really modest in their assessments. Zoltán Dörnyei: "With regard to my own influence, I suppose I have been influential in motivation research in general." Few would disagree.

## 2.11 Conclusion

In this project 106 applied linguists have provided information on a number of issues. The sample is probably not representative for the current AL population. In the sample there are many North Americans, a few British, and one or two representatives from various countries. Whole parts of the world are not represented. This may or may not be a problem. The fact is that, like in most other disciplines, the most important publications are written in English and for many of the informants, it is the only language they know.

There is a gender bias in that more men were invited as informants. In addition, men tend to list more men as leaders or authors of important publications than women, but that also holds for the female informants, though to a somewhat lower degree.

AL is largely a white discipline, and there is a remarkable absence of Afro-Americans in the field. There is a growing number of researchers with an Asian background who may become the leaders of the future.

The group of informants is also not representative in terms of age, because informants have been selected who have been active in the field during most of the period covered.

The informants show a wide range of educational backgrounds and the field is clearly not dominated by representatives from one or two programs or universities. A majority of the informants came to AL through teaching English as a Second Language (ESL) in the United States or Britain or English as a Foreign Language (EFL) in many countries in the world. Often the teaching experience led to an awareness of the need for a theoretical foundation of that teaching. This earlier experience with teaching ESL continues to have an impact on the populations studied in a considerable part of the research, where the focus on English is dominant.

The informants were also asked about who had influenced them and whom they had influenced. The names mentioned for the former question appeared to coincide largely with the leaders in the field they were asked to name. "Influence on" appeared to be a difficult question. Informants mention their graduate students or mutual influences with colleagues. No clear connection between "influenced by" and "influence on" could be established. Not all "influences on" were confirmed by those mentioned. This latter point makes it clear that the interviews and questionnaires did not produce all the information I was looking for. What I had in mind were lines of research over time traced through the links between generations of researchers.

The data gathered were to a certain extent saturated in the sense that additional interviews and questionnaire replies added less and less new information, but rather confirmed what other people had said before. So in that sense, for the questions asked this sample was sufficient, but of course the representativeness problem remains.

# References

Davies, A. and Elder, C. (2004) *The Handbook of Applied Linguistics*, Oxford: Blackwell.

Dörnyei, Z. (2012) *Motivation in Language Learning*, Shanghai: Shanghai Foreign Language Education Press.

Meara, P. (2012) "The bibliometrics of vocabulary acquisition: An exploratory study", *RELC Journal*, vol. 43, no. 1: 7–22.

Meara, P. (2014) "Vocabulary research in the *Modern Language Journal*: A bibliometric analysis", *Vocabulary Learning and Instruction*, advance online publication.

Thomas, M. (2013) "The doctorate in second language acquisition: An institutional history", *Linguistic Approaches to Bilingualism*, vol. 4, no. 1: 509–31.

# 3   Defining AL

What AL actually is, has been discussed intensively over the last decades, and despite these attempts no consensus has been reached. 1980 marked the start of the journal *Applied Linguistics* and in the first issues several applied linguists presented their views on what AL is and what, accordingly, the journal should be focused on. Widdowson's (1980) contribution "Models and fictions" continues to be influential in discussions on the scope of AL, and other publications, such as Corder (1973), Brumfit (1980), Grabe (2002), Davies and Elder (2004) and Kaplan (2010), have dealt with this in considerable detail. Widdowson took the issue up again in 2000, celebrating 20 years of the journal *Applied Linguistics* and in 2013 in the first issue of the *European Journal of Applied Linguistics*. In his view, "applied linguistics is concerned with language problems as experienced in the real world" (2000: 3). But he also mentions the question of who defines the problems. Not the applied linguist, who can easily create and solve the problem to his own satisfaction. Widdowson points out that there are many signs of AL as an independent discipline with its own institutions, conferences and journals, but he continues:

> In spite of all of this, there is a persistent and pervasive uncertainty about the name of the enquiry. Its institutional establishment as a name does not correspond with any very stable definition of just what it is. It is a phenomenon, one might mischievously suggest, a little like the Holy Roman Empire: a kind of convenient nominal fiction. This may be no bad thing, of course: indeed it is perhaps not in spite of, but *because* of this uncertainty that applied linguistics has flourished.
>
> (2000: 3)

The concern with real world problems is voiced eloquently by Weideman (1999):

> Applied linguists everywhere should be able to say to the world: here is assembled a group of dedicated experts, people informed both about the nature of language and about the acute problems accompanying the accessibility, acquisition, development, use and loss of language in our

daily lives. We are a group dedicated not to give final answers to many of these problems, but determined rather to employ what skills we have mastered to the benefit of those who need us most: the underprivileged, the destitute, the handicapped. We are determined to lead our discipline into avenues that are beneficial to mankind, something that advocates of "applied" science have sometimes miserably failed in doing.

(174)

## 3.1 An inclusive or exclusive definition?

There are two strands in the reactions of the informants, either an open one in line with the range of topics at the conferences of the Association Internationale de Linguistique Appliquée (AILA), or a more restricted one. The definitions of various AL organizations like AILA and AAAL (the American Association of Applied Linguistics) are often taken as a yardstick. The definitions of the field by both organizations can be found in Appendix 2.

Both these definitions try to be as inclusive as possible, avoiding any risk that someone would not feel welcome. This perspective is also reflected in the description of AL provided by Alan Davies and Cathy Elder, editors of *The Handbook of Applied Linguistics*:

> Applied linguistics is often said to be concerned with solving or at least ameliorating social problems involving language. The problems applied linguistics concerns itself with are likely to be: How can we teach languages better? How can we improve the training of translators and interpreters? How can we write a valid language examination? How can we evaluate a school bilingual program? How can we determine the literacy levels of a whole population? How can we helpfully discuss the language of a text? What advice can we offer a Ministry of Education on a proposal to introduce a new medium of instruction? How can we compare the acquisition of a European and an Asian language? What advice should we give a defense lawyer on the authenticity of a police transcript of an interview with a suspect?
>
> (Davies and Elder 2004: 1)

In her introduction to the monumental *Encyclopedia of Applied Linguistics*, Chapelle follows Hall *et al.* (2011: 19), who see AL

> as a mode of inquiry engaged with real people and issues arising in a political environment where academic perspectives and research alone may or may not be important in conceptualizing problems and finding solutions. In such an environment, problem solvers must genuinely engage with local knowledge and practice in seeking solutions.

Most of these authoritative definitions seem to argue for a broad and inclusive definition, and not for one that is purely restricted to the application of linguistic knowledge. Most of the informants who provide a definition of AL seem to agree with this. Susan Gass, a former AILA president, argues against a definition of AL that is too open. Her definition is: "AL is concerned with real life problems that can be solved with linguistic knowledge." William Grabe's: "AL addresses real world problems as they relate to discrimination, language learning problems, attrition, aging migrants, assessment and instruction and contact. These are all fundamental sources of problems."

Says Anne Burns:

> For me it has to do with using in-depth knowledge and theories of how language works to understand and contribute to a wide range of cultural and social contexts and behaviors. Also the diversification of paradigmatic and methodological approaches, and the development of these trends differently in different geographical locations.

But not all agree. For Michael Sharwood Smith, AL is "a very disparate field and I regard SLA, more familiar to me, as separate from applied linguistics, that is, it represents a field with explanation rather than application on its agenda". Stephen Krashen sees that differently:

> I don't think the term applied linguistics is accurate. To me it means that what we do is apply the results of grammatical theory, which we don't. Rather, I consider our work to be part of language acquisition. We are "applied" in the sense that our work has practical implications, but we are also concerned with theory at the same time. We are not involved in aspects of application that do not intersect with theory.

Anne Mauranen takes the following position:

> Applied linguistics means the study of language with its impact in mind: linguistics with a focus on issues where language is relevant to the lives of individuals and communities. In applied linguistics, many of the developments originated in trends in linguistic research, but in actual language education my impression is that the main trendsetter is educational, pedagogical thinking, and because applied linguistics originated in language teaching and learning, the pedagogical strain has remained strong.

The question is whether these different views are a real problem for the academic identity of AL. Reflecting on the need to define AL, Henry Widdowson continues: "One might take the view, of course, that people who call themselves applied linguists should stop agonizing about the nature of their enquiry, and just get on with it" (2000: 4). I tend to embrace this view and the one expressed by Eric Kellerman: "I think we can agree on what AL is by not defining it." Tove Skutnabb-Kangas feels the same. When asked what her definition of AL is she wrote: "I don't have one, and don't think it is important to define it."

However, for the present book that would not be very helpful since it would give no indication of who to approach for their views. As mentioned in the previous chapter, the definition of AL used for the present project is: the study of the development and use of multiple languages. I am very aware of the fact that this definition reflects my own history and preferences and is clearly not the generally accepted definition, though many of the interviewees seemed happy with it. But maybe that shows the bias in my selection of participants more than anything else. When I mentioned my definition to two of the founders of AAAL, Roger Shuy and Bernard Spolsky, their reactions were equivocal: "That's certainly not the definition that Henry Widdowson and I used when we started the journal [*Applied Linguistics*] in 1980!" (Spolsky), and:

> I should be clear that I don't disagree with your feeling that AAAL should be concerned with the development of multiple languages. That is certainly ONE of the important concerns AAAL should have. But I believe that my vision is much broader than that ... I feel that applied linguistics is stuck in a myopic definition of itself – language learning, teaching and testing.
>
> (Shuy)

It is interesting that in Roger Shuy's comments AAAL and AL seem to be equated. This is not uncommon. Joan Kelly Hall said: "When talking about applied linguistics it is hard to think outside AAAL", and Jodi Crandall takes it even a step further: "AAAL shaped AL." The link between AL and AAAL is generally seen as a strong one: almost all informants mention the annual AAAL conference as the conference they attend most regularly. When asked about leaders in the field Richard Young immediately thought of the past presidents of AAAL as the most important leaders.

While for Widdowson the development of AL is linked to the journal *Applied Linguistics*, for Catford (1998) there is a clear link between AL and the journal *Language Learning*. In his 'Language learning and applied linguistics: a historical sketch', he describes the development of AL from a largely American perspective. He mentions the customary developmental line from AL as language teaching and translation to a broader perspective that includes the range of topics that are now typically found in AL journals and conferences. He makes a remark on the use of the term "applied" that is relevant here:

> The adjective "applied" is more usually affixed to the names of sciences that have clearly acquired a recognized, independent existence as the study of their subject in and of itself, and thus contrast with "pure"

sciences which have become completely detached from the practical concerns that originally motivated most sciences.

(467)

This is to a certain extent also true of AL, which started as an attempt to create a scientific basis for language teaching. As Heidi Byrnes mentions, the need to gain respectability as a real science led to a focus on psycholinguistics that had already a high status and could serve as a stepping stone for AL to show its credibility. In her view that was a "false start" that continues to hound the field because it largely ignored the social and the emotional that is so pervasive in language learning. For Claire Kramsch the impact of psycholinguistics was a positive development. For a long time the applied linguists and other people involved in language teaching were "the plumbers" in language and literature departments, and they had little prestige. "The Mike Longs of this world have given AL the respectability it now has. The hard core, quantitative, statistically reliable data, not the messy post-structural stuff." Lyle Bachman in this context refers to "the relative credibility" of AL as an academic discipline. Chris Candlin makes an interesting socio-geographical comparison: "AL is like Portugal, looking outward only!"

The inferiority syndrome is also mentioned by Henry Widdowson, in particular with respect to the early emphasis on language learning and teaching, which is "not terribly prestigious". Therefore, taking notions and theories from academic disciplines with a better pedigree helps to enhance the status of the field. But in his view that hinders the engagement with real world problems. Chris Candlin is characteristically open about his views on this: "Applied linguistics as solving real world problems? I don't like solving by experts, it can only come from joint participation."

All descriptions of the development of AL discuss the relation between AL and linguistics, or, more specifically, theoretical linguistics. While in the old days, the 1950s until the late 1970s, linguistics was seen as the main scientific basis for AL, the gap between them has been growing ever since. "For the contribution of linguistics to language teaching we have to remember," says Lyle Bachman, "that the old Fries/Lado approach, usually referred to as the audio-lingual method, was based on American structural linguistics, which grew out of extensive empirical research with 'Amerindian' languages. The same cannot be said about current input from linguistics".

Widdowson (1980, 2000) makes a distinction between AL as concerned with language related real world problems and "linguistics applied" as an approach in which "the assumption is that the problem can be reformulated by the unique and unilateral application of concepts and terms derived from linguistic enquiry itself" (5). William Grabe agrees:

Linguistics applied makes no sense to me. We are not linguists applying linguistic knowledge. The idea that a, or every, linguist could be an applied linguist makes no sense to me. We all bring knowledge from some area(s) outside of linguistics as well to address language-related issues.

Alastair Pennycook sees a continued struggle with identity: "AL is still asking itself what it is and how it relates to linguistics, though it has started to come of age and see itself as a discipline in itself rather than continue to struggle with the linguistics applied label."

The problem is that there is no consensus in the field on what kind of linguistics might be applied. During the period covered here, Chomsky's Universal Grammar (UG) was overall the leading linguistic model, but researchers using this paradigm were not primarily interested in applications. As Lydia White mentions in her reaction to the question "to what extent and if so, how has AL research led to an improvement of language education?": "Research findings do not necessarily have direct applications."

In recent years, we have seen the growth of approaches to language that can best be labeled as "usage based". What these approaches have in common is that no innate language capacity is assumed or seen as necessary, since the input in language learning is rich enough and complexity can emerge from the interaction of simple procedures. This type of linguistics is much more amenable to views of language as a social construct. The focus on the social also means that AL as aimed at language problems as experienced in the real world, can more easily contribute to such problems.

The strict distinction between theoretical linguistics and AL favored by a majority of the informants is not shared by everyone. In reaction to the invitation to participate in the study, Antonella Sorace mentions: "I'd be happy to participate, though I regard myself as an eclectic bridge builder and I've never liked labels like 'applied linguistics' and 'theoretical linguistics'."

Over the years, not only the relation between linguistics and AL changed. Also the foci in research changed. Suresh Canagarajah says:

> In its conception AL was very cognitive, as you can see in the early literature such as Corder (1976). My own view changed, as did the field. Now it is connected to migration studies, ethnography, identity issues, from teaching to more multi-disciplinarity. Earlier modernist controlled experiments are now less important. Now it is more post modern, which includes studying values and a role for researcher's views.

The change Canagarajah refers to is often referred to as "the social turn", a term originally coined by Block (2003), but for many informants linked to the Firth and Wagner article of 2007 in *The Modern Language Journal*. This is seen as a watershed in AL over the last decades. The article seemed to have said what so many applied linguists could not or did not dare to say according to Heidi Byrnes. When asked why the Firth and Wagner article had such an impact, Karin Johnson said that it was "possibly a liberation of the psycholinguistic chains that reduced the human to an information processing system". To Jim Lantolf the whole discussion generated by the Firth and Wagner article was frustrating, because as he said: "we [people working in a sociocultural approach] had made the turn already or, rather, it wasn't a change because the cognitive and the social are always connected in SCT."

## 3.2 The autonomy of AL

One of the issues with defining AL is whether it can stand on its own, taking from other disciplines as much as giving to them. Some informants feel that AL is still taking more than it gives. Suresh Canagarajah disagrees: "AL is no longer a stepchild of linguistics; AL doesn't only borrow from other fields. We have tools and theories that are relevant for sociology." But still, applied linguists do borrow heavily from other disciplines; from education to neuro-imaging and from ethnography to power analysis in statistics. This may not be a weakness, even though it makes the position of AL as an independent discipline weaker.

## 3.3 Unity, fragmentation or compartmentalization?

As will be discussed in Chapters 6 and 7 on major trends, many informants refer to what some call fragmentation and others more positively as compartmentalization. Claire Kramsch even states: "What defines AL most, is its openness to influences from outside." According to Gabriele Kasper the compartmentalization of AL is not a weakness, but a sign of maturity. Just like other branches of science, AL will diversify. Worldwide, we see that what used to be core science (e.g. psychology, biology) is now compartmen-talized (social psychology, neuropsychology/socio-biology, marine biology). "AL is a broad church. The field should be open to new sub-disciplines to grow within the system and become more independent over time." She sees testing as a good example; it used to be one of the core components of AL, but branched out and became more or less independent with its own con-ferences, journals and books. It is not desirable to fight such developments. At the same time, there should be a dialogue between the branches, since they have many intersections. Gabriele Kasper sees her own interest in oral testing and conversational analysis (CA) as an example. Another advantage of this specialization, she mentions, is that it allows students to choose: stu-dents interested in Socio-Cultural Theory (SCT) opt for the AL program at Pennsylvania State University, while students interested in cognitive proces-sing opt for the program at the University of Maryland.

Howard Nicholas says:

> I do not think that applied linguistics is comfortably singular. The ideo-logical and content differences are enormous and so it is at best a loose coalition of overlapping interests, where even the reasons for the coalition (applied linguistics vs. linguistics applied) are contested.

Dick Schmidt noticed: "Loss of focus and compartmentalization into sub-disciplines (small communities) with little communication among them, e.g., the generativists, the conversation analysts, etc." Alastair Pennycook sees "the rise of SLA theory and its subsequent separation into an almost separate area of work". As mentioned earlier, for some informants (Henry Widdowson, Barbara Seidlhofer, Michael Sharwood Smith) SLA is not even part of AL.

With respect to the interaction with other disciplines, Gabriele Kasper contends:

> We don't only take, we also give, though the uptake is not great. Raising the awareness of the impact of multilingualism is input for other fields, such as sociology, psychology and education in which a monolingual attitude is still the norm.

## 3.4 AL and TESOL

The relationship between AL and TESOL (Teachers of English to Speakers of Other Languages) is in fact the relationship between AAAL and TESOL. After splitting off from the Linguistic Society of America (LSA), AAAL teamed up for a couple of years with TESOL by having their conferences next to each other in the same city, allowing participants to take part in both conferences. This was the case from 1991 until 2003 and in 2011 until 2014. There are no hard data on participation that would support the idea that many people would attend both conferences. There is a fairly clear division of labor between the two organizations: TESOL is primarily aimed at the teaching of English as a second or foreign language and research is not the focus, while AAAL aims at both English and other languages and is more research oriented. Over the years, attempts to increase the number of research papers at TESOL conferences have largely failed and informal estimates on the basis of the programs of both conferences suggest that the group of academics partaking in both is fairly small. However, AAAL is still predominantly about English: based on the information in the abstracts, a count of the paper presentations at AAAL 2014 in Portland showed that out of a total of 844 papers, 387 (46 percent) were on the learning, teaching or use of English, 163 (19 percent) were on other languages than English, while 294 (35 percent) were not aimed at a specific language. It seems that foreign language activity is still more the domain of the American Council on the Teaching of Foreign Languages (ACTFL).

## 3.5 AL and AILA

AILA is basically an association of national associations, and has no individual membership. The AILA congress takes place every three years and the aim is to organize the congress in different parts of the world. Organizers pay a fee to AILA, and are responsible for the financial side. Any profit they make is theirs, but losses have to be covered as well. The acceptance rate for AILA congresses has been rather high traditionally, which may be the result of both a sense of inclusiveness and financial considerations. AILA is an official NGO having FCR (Formal Consultative Relations) with UNESCO. It publishes a book series with John Benjamins Publishers and the *AILA Review* with the same publisher and until recently was associated with the journal *Applied Linguistics*.

Because AILA has no individual fee-paying members and only receives a nominal fee per participant of the world congresses, the financial means, and therefore the impact on the field, are extremely limited. Several informants indicate that it is useful to have a world organization, but wonder what AILA actually does. It clearly has no formative role to play in any other international organization.

The majority of the informants in this study, as far as they ventured to provide a definition of AL, seem to opt for a broad definition of AL that focuses on real world problems that can be solved with linguistic means. At the same time most of them seemed happy with the definition I used. Here is what some of the informants mentioned:

PAUL ANGELIS:   "Applied linguistics represents a constellation of theory, research and practice flowing from a number of social sciences which affect and influence language in all of its manifestations."

GUY COOK:   "The boundaries of applied linguistics are very vague. For example, people working in corpus linguistics and stylistics (two very important areas for me) may not regard themselves as applied linguists. Secondly, if I confine myself to 'mainstream' applied linguistics, then I have not generally been influenced by people and publications from it much at all! In fact, I generally have a very low opinion of it, especially SLA which I regard as lacking rigor and depth. The biggest influences on my work have been from outside 'mainstream' applied linguistics which I have used to inform my own work. These include: literary theory, play theory, media studies, semiotics, food politics, translation studies and the philosophy of biology."

DURK GORTER:   "Applied linguistics consists of all the (sub-) fields that the AILA conferences cover."

BERND RÜSSCHOFF:   "In AILA, we point out that applied linguistics is an interdisciplinary field of research and practice dealing with practical problems of language, language learning, language use and communication. It differs from linguistics in general mainly with respect to its explicit orientation towards practical, everyday problems related to language and communication as well as its focus on robust and informed solutions of problems identified. To me, it is important to keep in mind that, despite its origins in language acquisition and language teaching, AL has grown into a field which is concerned with any aspect of language and of how language is used and functions in all walks of professional, institutional and personal life."

PAUL MEARA: "Those bits of linguistics which are not directly concerned with describing language in the abstract."

ELIZABETH LANZA: "A very broad one. Various theoretical and practical approaches to the study of language in use. Note that 'applied' linguistics can also be theoretical!"

ANTONELLA SORACE: "Linguistics related to the real world."

ANNE BURNS: "For me it's to do with using in-depth knowledge and theories of how language works to understand and contribute to a wide range of cultural and social contexts and behaviours."

## 3.6 Conclusion

Summarizing we can say that there are roughly three tendencies in defining AL. One is that AL is concerned with real world problems and ways to solve them on the basis of linguistic knowledge and tools. For the representatives of this definition, subfields like SLA are not part of AL because they do not primarily deal with real world problems. The second is that AL largely overlaps with SLA. For this group of researchers, the real world problems are not the defining component. AL is seen as a research field that makes use of a variety of research techniques and tools and is primarily empirical in nature. The third type of definition is the widest one: AL is everything that has to do with language apart from theoretical linguistics.

My own definition comes closest to the AL = SLA one. It is a fairly limiting definition that refers to a rather close-knit network of researchers that could be said to form a community of practice: there are special books and journals, conferences and shared views on methodology. Whether that is in fact true remains to be proven. Many of my informants are working in the area of SLA, so what follows is biased in that sense. Many areas that for representatives of the other perspectives would typically be AL are not, or are only marginally, covered.

Looking back, it might have been better to give informants my definition up front and ask them about their views on this. I did this a couple of times and that seemed to work well. At any rate some of the informants agreed with me that my definition and the real world problems one are not mutually exclusive, but rather complementary. Many applied linguists work on real world problems that have to do with multiple languages. Several of them mentioned the now highly relevant issue of asylum seekers in many parts of the world. Language issues and knowledge about how languages can vary over time and between individuals are very important, in particular when proficiency in particular languages play a role in the decision to grant an asylum seeker a permit to live and work in the receiving country or not.

So, though there are three ways to define AL, adhering to one does not exclude the others. In the remaining chapters different types of data are presented that bear on the question of how to define AL. Do the informants see the same individuals as the leaders of the field, and is there a core literature in journal articles and books that defines the field? Do applied linguists publish in specific journals and with specific publishers?

# References

Block, D. (2003) *The Social Turn in Second Language Acquisition*, Edinburgh: Edinburgh University Press.

Brumfit, C. (1980) "From defining to designing: Communicative specifications versus communicative methodology in foreign language teaching", *Studies in Second Language Acquisition*, vol. 3, no. 1: 1–9.

Catford, J. (1998) "Language learning and applied linguistics: a historical sketch", *Language Learning*, vol. 48, no. 4: 465–96.

Chapelle, C. (2014) *The Encyclopedia of Applied Linguistics*, New York: Wiley.

Corder, S. Pit (1973) *Introducing Applied Linguistics*, London: Penguin Longman.

Davies, A. and Elder, C. (2004) *The Handbook of Applied Linguistics*, Oxford: Blackwell.

Firth, A. and Wagner, J. (2007) "Second/foreign language learning as a social accomplishment: Elaborations on a reconceptualized SLA", *The Modern Language Journal*, vol. 91: 800–19.

Grabe, W. (2002) "Applied linguistics: An emerging discipline for the twenty-first century" in: R. Kaplan (ed.) *The Oxford Handbook of Applied Linguistics*, Oxford: Oxford University Press, pp. 3–12.

Hall, C., Smith, P. and Wicaksono, R. (2011) *Mapping Applied Linguistics: A Guide for Students and Practitioners*, New York: Routledge.

Kaplan, R. (ed.) (2010) *The Oxford Handbook of Applied Linguistics*, 2nd edn, Oxford: Oxford University Press.

Weideman, A. (1999) "Five generations of applied linguistics: Some framework issues", *Acta Academia*, vol. 31, no. 1: 77–98.

Widdowson, H. (1980) "Models and fictions", *Applied Linguistics*, vol. 1, no. 2: 165–70.

Widdowson, H. (2000) "On the limits of linguistics applied", *Applied Linguistics*, vol. 21, no. 1: 3–25.

Widdowson, H. (2013) "On the applicability of empirical findings", *European Journal of Applied Linguistics* vol. 1, no. 1: 4–21.

# 4  The leaders

The item in the questionnaire on leaders was: "Who are the most important/ influential leaders in the field? Why are they important?" Though the question was formulated in the present tense, many informants referred to academics long retired or dead. No specific definition of what constitutes a leader was given, and as the responses show, there was a variety of definitions.

## 4.1 Criteria for leaders

As Howard Nicholas correctly observes, the assumption behind this question is that there is "a clear sense of a single field" that has leaders. As we have seen in Chapter 2, this is not the perception of all informants. So, like Susan Gass, Paul Nation, William Grabe, Rod Ellis and Gabriele Kasper, he sees no leaders for the whole field, but rather for the different compartments, which are not clearly defined themselves. Both William Grabe and Susan Gass said: "There is no Chomsky in AL."

In a way Patricia Duff agrees when she says:

> Currently there are many (100+) leaders in the field since it has expanded in so many areas and deepened over the years. There are important thinkers, dynamic high-visibility speakers, prolific scholars, and devoted leaders (not all of them can do all of these things equally well, or should) who have slogged away as journal editors and association presidents etc., for many years.

This view is also expressed by Martin Bygate who sees this as a fairly recent development:

> Up until the second half of the 1990s, although there were distinct strands, this [listing leaders] was relatively easy to say, though direction and influences changed every seven years or so. Since then, the field has fragmented significantly, and it has become harder (for me at least) to identify clear influential leaders. So instead the question perhaps becomes

"who are the influential leaders in the various fields or subfields of applied linguistics"?

Still, most informants mentioned people who they see as leaders. Not everyone indicated what his or her criteria were for this. Peter Robinson feels that "apart from being very good at explaining what they write about, these people are also very productive, and constructive". The constructive attitude is also foregrounded by Merrill Swain, for whom it is hard to separate the academic from the person. Bluntly carrying out a personal agenda and offending people deeply are not what characterizes leaders for her, even when they are effective in getting the research done. Elaine Tarone defines them as "people who question authority", Lourdes Ortega defines leaders as people who are willing to change their views, who can read the Zeitgeist and are willing to leave certitudes of an established position behind; "people who have at least two momentums in their career". Heidi Byrnes agrees:

> Leaders are people who are willing and able to change position if needed. You need legitimacy to change your position, it is not simple flip-flopping, but there may be changes at different levels that call for a re-analysis of the present situation.

Andrew Cohen uses the term "shakers" to define leaders; people who move things forward. According to Diane Larsen-Freeman, leaders are characterized by their academic integrity, sense of social justice and breadth of perspective. Zoltán Dörnyei says of leaders: "They all pushed the field forward by introducing contemporary theories from related disciplines in the social sciences as well as by setting international standards." For John Schumann leaders are "thinkers, researchers and officers".

While academic standing is an agreed upon characteristic, there is less agreement on whether such leaders should also be active as organizers of conferences, officers in professional organizations, be connected to relevant governmental organizations and the like. For Merrill Swain, "real leaders bring academic weight but also a contribution to the AL community in terms of being active in organizing conferences, editorships of books and journals and other activities". For Richard Young, officers in large professional organizations like AAAL (American Association of Applied Linguistics) are leaders, in particular the presidents, but there is a bias: "The problem with this method is that they are (or were) all North American." William Grabe does not agree that the AAAL presidents are by definition leaders; he comments that some of the presidents are not really part of the community, since they never come to AAAL's annual conferences. "Nominating committees don't seem to take into account who are regular attendants of the conference. It is not enough to be an outstanding academic or respected colleague. Some continued commitment to the field and the community should weigh similarly." With respect to the AAAL leadership, John Schumann argues that having a high profile president may enhance the status of the field even when that person is not the typical applied linguist or a regular AAAL conference-goer. In his view, having someone like Michael Tomasello as president would be good for the profile of the field while such a person clearly would not define himself as an applied linguist.

## 4.2 The list of leaders

Not surprisingly, most of the informants who were interviewed only had a quick look at the questionnaire before the interview, but Alan Juffs was a laudable exception; he mailed his responses even before the interview. The impromptu listing of names is not ideal. As Lourdes Ortega remarked, it is a bit like a verbal fluency task in which the participant has to name as many birds or words beginning with an "s" in one or two minutes. As with the verbal fluency task, participants had different strategies to come up with names. Some listed people on the basis of geography, others of topics or publications. I started out asking people to list names and give reasons for their choices, but I would also suggest names to which they were free to say yes or no. This may have led to a bias in favor of the best known people, though the names suggested were sometimes also focusing on specific lines of research.

This question clearly left quite some room for listing many different people, also because "the field" was not uniformly defined. Even adding my own definition (the development and use of multiple languages) didn't lead to a restriction of people who were active in the area at all. Many informants listed researchers who would not be typically called applied linguists, such as Bourdieu, Goffman or Perfetti. I decided that all names mentioned in the interviews would simply be listed. The scattering of names is of course a sign of the links to many other different fields of research that applied linguists make use of, but may also be a sign of a lack of focus. As mentioned in the previous chapter, interdisciplinarity is clearly a main characteristic of our field.

All the names were put in an Excel file that generated a frequency count of the people mentioned. The total set of names mentioned consists of 228 individuals. This set has been reduced by removing the names that were mentioned three times or less. Table 4.1 shows the frequency of listing of the names mentioned at least four times.

The list in Table 4.1 allows us to define the leaders in our field. There are 58 names mentioned at least four times. The frequency distribution shows a clear top group consisting of:

- Claire Kramsch
- Merrill Swain
- James Lantolf
- Diane Larsen-Freeman.

*Table 4.1* List of leaders with number of times mentioned

| | | | |
|---|---|---|---|
| Kramsch | 37 | Brumfit | 7 |
| Swain | 37 | Byrnes | 7 |
| Lantolf | 31 | Cook, G. | 7 |
| Larsen-Freeman | 30 | Duff | 7 |
| Long | 23 | Hatch | 7 |
| Widdowson | 23 | Lightbown | 7 |
| Ellis, N. | 22 | Richards | 7 |
| De Bot | 19 | Lambert, W. | 7 |
| Gass | 19 | Blommaert | 6 |
| Corder | 14 | Canagarajah | 6 |
| Krashen | 14 | Cohen | 6 |
| Candlin | 13 | Hyltenstam | 6 |
| Halliday | 13 | Kasper | 6 |
| Ortega | 13 | Pienemann | 6 |
| Cummins | 12 | Trim | 6 |
| Spolsky | 11 | Ferguson | 5 |
| Ellis, R. | 11 | Kellerman | 5 |
| Dörnyei | 10 | Meisel | 5 |
| Pavlenko | 10 | Rampton | 5 |
| Schumann | 10 | Selinker | 5 |
| Tucker | 10 | Cook, V. | 5 |
| DeKeyser | 9 | Chapelle | 4 |
| Hymes | 9 | Clyne | 4 |
| McNamara | 9 | Gregg | 4 |
| Pennycook | 9 | Johnson, Keith | 4 |
| Tarone | 9 | Meara | 4 |
| Hulstijn | 8 | Norton | 4 |
| Shohamy | 8 | Ochs | 4 |
| White | 8 | Stevick | 4 |
| Bachman | 7 | | |

Then the numbers drop gradually with a long tail of less frequently mentioned individuals. There are 17 women in the list and 41 men, but three out of the five leaders listed most are women. Of the 58 individuals, there are 35 from the United States or Canada, nine from the UK, four from the Netherlands, four Australians, two Israelis, one New Zealander, one from Japan, one German and one Swede. Americans tend to list fellow countrymen; non-Americans tend to list relatively more non-Americans.

The data show that, on the one hand, there is a small group of applied linguists who are considered to be the main leaders in the field, which could be interpreted as a sign that AL is a field guided by some authoritative leaders. On the other hand, there is a very large group of individuals who are also mentioned as leaders. So the group of informants stating that there are no leaders may be wrong here to a certain extent. It was also suggested that there might be different fields, each with their own leader. Looking at the list, some names can be linked to subfields, like Selinker to interlanguage and Tarone to variation, but many of the individuals listed have been working on various topics and have had various momentums, as Lourdes Ortega remarked in her definition of what constitutes a leader. In the list there are also applied linguists who had an impact historically, but have passed away, like Ferguson, Hymes, Wallace Lambert, Trim and Pit Corder, or now no longer play a role, like Kellerman and Richard Lambert. In that sense, the list is not a reflection of who are the leaders at present, rather it indicates the leaders over the last 30 years, as listed by the informants.

As mentioned before, detailed information about age is not available, but the average age seems to be in the 55–65 range. Many younger researchers are taking over the role of the older generation and will be the leaders of the next generation. This includes people like Lourdes Ortega, Aneta Pavlenko, Jean-Marc Dewaele and Marianne Gullberg.

As mentioned in the previous chapter, the majority of the leaders in the list are men. In addition, men tend to list more men than women as leaders, and women do the same.

## 4.3  Portraits of the main leaders

In this section short portraits of the main leaders (mentioned ten times or more) are presented in order of number of listings based on the comments by the informants. Their main lines of research are presented, followed by comments from the informants and a listing of their two most frequently cited publications.

### Claire Kramsch

Claire Kramsch's work focuses on the relation between language and language teaching in context. She emphasizes the role of culture and literature and thereby connects ideas from various scholars from various countries, including Germany and France.

"She has been a huge presence over the last 20 years, pushing our thinking in new directions, urging us to understand." "She knows about AL outside the Anglo world, presenting important ideas about multilingualism." "She is tireless, passionate and engaged." "She started looking at ecological aspects of AL long before anyone else."

She is currently president of AILA and a former president of AAAL.

Kramsch, C. (1993) *Context and Culture in Language Teaching*, Oxford: Oxford University Press.

Kramsch, C. (1998) *Language and Culture*, Oxford: Oxford University Press.

### Merrill Swain

Merrill Swain's work ranges from evaluation of immersion education to language and aging and sociocultural aspects of language learning and teaching. She developed the output-hypothesis as a reaction to Krashen's input-hypothesis.

"She is to be admired for her versatility and long-term commitment to applied linguistics scholarship." "She had the guts to change her mind about the foundational assumptions of her research AFTER she had already become a universally celebrated scholar in our field." "Critical but fair, she has influenced many researchers in our field by setting a high standard for both quantitative and qualitative research." "Very supportive for upcoming young researchers and graduate students." "For her work on communicative competence, the output-hypothesis and the relevance of languaging as a source of SLA."

She is a former president of AAAL.

Canale, M. and Swain, M. (1980) "Theoretical bases of communicative approaches to second language teaching and testing", *Applied Linguistics*, vol. 1, no. 1: 1–47.

Swain, M. (1995) "Three functions of output in second language learning" in: B. Seidlhofer and G. Cook (eds), *Principle and Practice in Applied Linguistics: Studies in Honour of H.G. Widdowson*, Oxford: Oxford University Press, pp. 125–44.

### James Lantolf

Originally a dissatisfied secondary school teacher, who later earned a degree in historical linguistics and who also researched Spanish dialects in the United States. He gradually developed an interest in the work of Vygotsky and other Russian educational psychologists and is now seen as the leading figure in the SCT movement.

"He is a brilliant scholar with a deep knowledge of many aspects of the field." "He has been very influential in articulating an alternative to the narrow SLA position held by some, and in developing a major program that develops and supports this view." "He has more or less single handedly generated a new branch of AL, through his tireless defense and illustration of Vygotskian sociocultural theory." "He is a loyal friend and mentor."

He is a former president of AAAL.

Lantolf, J. (ed.) (2000) *Sociocultural Theory and Second Language Learning*, Oxford: Oxford University Press.

Lantolf, J. and Thorne, S. (2006) *Sociocultural Theory and the Genesis of Second Language Development*, Oxford: Oxford University Press.

### Diane Larsen-Freeman

Diane Larsen-Freeman's work ranges from grammar teaching to various aspects of second language acquisition and more recently the application of complexity theory to SLA.

"She is a stalwart of the field, who has worked on an amazing range of topics." "Her work on grammaring has been very influential and her book with Michael Long served to define the field of AL." "Recently livening things up with her promotion of complexity theory." "She is a pioneer and thinks outside the box." "She triggered debates on the dynamic nature of inter-languages." "She is one of the few applied linguists who have worked on both teaching practices and fundamental research." "She bridges the gap between theory and practice like nobody else." "She is much more open minded than many of her American colleagues; open to questioning her own findings."

Larsen-Freeman, D. (1997) "Chaos/complexity science and second language acquisition", *Applied Linguistics*, vol. 18, no. 2: 141–65.

Larsen-Freeman, D. and Long, M. (1991) *An Introduction to Second Language Acquisition Research*, New York: Longman.

## Michael Long

Michael Long's work covers a wide range of topics related to focus on form/ forms, and the role of the linguistic environment. He has been a strong defender of the critical period hypothesis. He was the symbol of the mod-ernist/cognitive approach to SLA along with his colleagues in Hawaii for a long time.

"Promoter of the interaction hypothesis and of research on instructed language learning/'focus on form'." "Very productive and prolific in his writings." "Edited the influential *Handbook of Second Language Acquisition* with Catherine Doughty." "Sometimes relentless in his views on other applied linguists, but a source of inspiration for many."

Long, M. (1983) "Native speaker/non-native speaker conversation and the negotiation of comprehensible input", *Applied Linguistics*, vol. 4, no. 2: 126–41.

Long, M.H. (1996) "The role of the linguistic environment in second language acquisition" in: W.C. Ritchie and T.K. Bahtia (eds), *Handbook of Second Language Acquisition*, New York: Academic Press, pp. 413–68. Reprinted in L. Ortega (ed.), *Second Language Acquisition: Critical Concepts in Linguistics*, London: Routledge.

## Henry Widdowson

Henry Widdowson has been a highly influential contributor to the commu-nicative language teaching movement through his promotion of functional perspectives on language. He has had an impact on both sides of the Atlantic and worked on Content and Language Integrated Learning (CLIL) and English for Special Purposes (ESP) well before it became fashionable.

"He is an independent thinker and a brilliant speaker in the British tradition." "Helped develop a coherent model of communicative language teaching." "For his theorizing of the discipline, his work on discourse analysis and stylistics, his rigorous critiques, and his exposure of muddled thinking." "A key figure in communicative language teaching as well as critical discourse analysis, as well as his considerations concerning global English." "His writings go to the essence of the issue and he puts his fingers on the sour point." "Very influential through his advisorship with *Oxford University Press*."

Widdowson, H. (1978) *Teaching Language as Communication*, Oxford: Oxford University Press.

Widdowson, H. (1984) *Explorations in Applied Linguistics*, Oxford: Oxford University Press.

### Nick Ellis

Nick Ellis works from a usage based perspective and concentrates on the role of frequency in SLA and the role of implicit and explicit language knowledge. He is one of the leading researchers working on emergentism in language learning.

"He is provocative and rigorous and brings together data from a range of fields and connects them elegantly." "He brings a cognitive linguistics perspective to AL that fills the gap with the decline of more formal linguistic theories." "He offers a plausible theory of SLA, and also does excellent work in several other areas of AL."

Ellis, N. (1996) "Sequencing in SLA", *Studies in Second Language Acquisition*, vol. 18, no. 1: 91–126.

Ellis, N. (2002) "Frequency effects in language processing", *Studies in Second Language Acquisition*, vol. 24, no. 2: 143–88.

### Kees de Bot

Kees de Bot worked on a number of topics, including bilingual language production, language attrition, language and aging and the application of DST to language development and multilingualism.

"He introduced an L2 version of Levelt's speaking model, something the field was waiting for." "More recently he has been influential in shifting the study of SLA to complexity."

De Bot, K. (1992) "A bilingual production model: Levelt's speaking model adapted", *Applied Linguistics*, vol. 13, no. 1: 1–24.

De Bot, K., Lowie, W. and Verspoor, M. (2007) "A dynamic systems theory approach to second language acquisition", *Bilingualism: Language and Cognition*, vol. 10, no. 1: 7–21.

### Susan Gass

Susan Gass has published a number of books on research methodology and SLA. She has done research on various topics, including input and interaction, negotiation of meaning in native–non-native interaction and language transfer.

"She is an amazingly productive researcher and author on SLA and research methods." "Her work on interaction has been hugely influential."

"She was influential in the integration of linguistic theory and second language acquisition." "In later years, Gass and Mackey's work in research design is important."

She was president of AILA for three years and a former president of AAAL.

Gass, S. (2013) *Input, Interaction and the Second Language Learner*, New York: Routledge.

Gass, S. (2013) *Second Language Acquisition: An Introductory Course*, New York: Routledge.

### Stephen Pit Corder

Pit Corder, who passed away in 1990, was a founding figure in SLA. He popularized the idea of "interlanguage" and made the AL community aware of the significance of learner errors. He co-edited the famous Edinburgh series that paved the way for AL to develop.

"He alerted the field to the creative nature of 'errors'." "He was a source of inspiration for a whole generation." "He has been influential through his cooperation with many researchers who later became leaders in the field."

Corder, S. P. (1967) "The significance of learner's errors", *International Review of Applied Linguistics in Language Teaching*, vol. 5, no. 1–4: 161–70.

Corder, S. (1981) *Error Analysis and Interlanguage*, Oxford: Oxford University Press.

### Stephen Krashen

Stephen Krashen started out as a neurolinguist but has been extremely influential through his work on the natural approach to language teaching. His book *Principles and Practice of Second Language Acquisition* is mentioned frequently as one of the most influential books in the last decades. His recent work is on advocacy for minority language users.

"Stephen Krashen and Tracy Terrell strove to let the world know that learning second languages was 'natural'." "Knows how to make research relevant for teachers." "Captivating speaker." "An activist in minority language education."

Krashen, S. (1981) *Second Language Acquisition and Second Language Learning*, Oxford: Oxford University Press.

Krashen, S. (1982) *Principles and Practice in Second Language Acquisition*, Oxford: Pergamon.

### Chris Candlin

Chris Candlin promoted communicative language teaching through various publications. His more recent interests lie in the use of language teaching in professional communities for which he works, for example healthcare professionals. Rather than through his own research and publications, he has possibly been most influential through his role as book editor, which is much underrated. He has also articulated an important position on AL in relation to professional practices.

"A brilliant editor and as someone who spots promising people early, a stimulator with a sense of development of what is emergent. Good antenna for what is likely to be the next thing." "He knows how to manage people in different ways."

He was president of AILA for six years.

Breen, M. and Candlin, C. (1980) "The essentials of a communicative curriculum in language teaching", *Applied Linguistics*, vol. 1, no. 2: 89–112.

Candlin, C. (2002) *Research and Practice in Professional Discourse*, Hong Kong: City University of Hong Kong Press.

## Michael Halliday

Michael Halliday is the founder of Systemic Functional Grammar (SFG), which has had a substantial impact on AL, in particular in Australia, but also in a number of universities in the United States and the UK. He argued for a connection between social structures and language at a time when language was mainly seen as a cognitive phenomenon.

Halliday, M. and Hasan, R. (2014) *Cohesion in English*, New York: Routledge.

Halliday, M. and Matthiesen, C. (2014) *An Introduction to Functional Grammar*, New York: Routledge.

## Lourdes Ortega

Lourdes Ortega is one of the upcoming researchers in AL. Her meta-analysis (with John Norris) of form-focused instruction is one of the most important studies in AL in the last decades. She also wrote an introductory text on SLA. She is the main editor of the journal *Language Learning*.

"She is an excellent methodologist, promoter of systematic reviews, also committed to steering AL toward a focus on multilingualism." "As general editor of *Language Learning* she is very supportive of upcoming young researchers." "Few match her on knowledge of the field, both historical and current."

Norris, J. and Ortega, L. (2000) "Effectiveness of L2 instruction: A research synthesis and quantitative meta-analysis", *Language Learning*, vol. 50, no. 3: 417–528.

Ortega, L. (1999) "Planning and focus on form in L2 oral performance", *Studies in Second Language Acquisition*, vol. 21, no. 1: 109–48.

## James Cummins

James Cummins is best known for his work on Cognitive Academic Language Proficiency (CALP), Basic Interpersonal Communicative Skills (BICS) and his theory of underlying language proficiency ("Cummins' Iceberg"). He also works on literacy in bilingual settings.

"Influential in research on teaching of minority language children." "Does sustainable research." "Knows how to talk to teachers."

Cummins, J. (1978) "Bilingualism and the developments of metalinguistic awareness", *Journal of Cross-Cultural Psychology*, vol. 9, no. 2: 131–49.

Cummins, J. (1979) "Linguistic interdependence and the educational development of bilingual children", *Review of Educational Research*, vol. 49, no. 2: 222–51.

### Bernard Spolsky

Bernard Spolsky's interests and publications are wide-ranging: from language policy to sociolinguistics, language management and language testing. He was involved in setting up the journal *Applied Linguistics*.

"He has been an acting force on many levels and in a variety of research areas." "A deep thinker that had a major impact on the awareness of the ethics of language testing." "His 1989 book on foundational aspects of language learning is mentioned frequently as one of the most important publications of that era."

Former president of TESOL.

Spolsky, B. (1989) *Conditions for Second Language Learning: Introduction to a General Theory*, Oxford: Oxford University Press.

Spolsky, B. (2004) *Language Policy*, Cambridge: Cambridge University Press.

### Rod Ellis

Rod Ellis is involved in research that relates SLA research and actual language teaching. He has also worked on task-based language learning and teaching. His book *The Study of Second Language Acquisition*, which first appeared in 1994, has received regular updates and is probably the most cited book in the field of AL.

"He is an amazingly productive reviewer and encyclopedist. He defined the field and keeps it informed about SLA research and about language classroom research. Also a leading figure in task-based learning and teaching and in grammar pedagogy." "He is consequential and had impact through his books and lectures all over the world." "His work has been so encompassing and it has dealt with so many aspects of SLA that it would be difficult to even provide a list." "He calls himself an empiricist rather than a modernist."

Ellis, R. (1994/2013) *The Study of Second Language Acquisition*, Oxford: Oxford University Press.

Ellis, R. (2003) *Task-based Language Learning and Teaching*, Oxford: Oxford University Press.

## Zoltán Dörnyei

Zoltán Dörnyei is a leading figure in research on individual differences, in particular regarding motivation and attitudes. He has developed conceptual models of motivation that can be applied to language teaching in classrooms, but is also firmly based in research on motivation outside of AL. In addition to his books on motivation he published on research methodology, the use of surveys and the psychology of the language learner.

"His challenge to the big name in the field of motivation, Robert Gardner, was ultimately successful, and his 'future L2 self' perspective has become dominant in motivation research." "Recently he started applying DST to motivational aspects of language learning." "He is incredibly productive, producing one book after the other, and all high quality."

Dörnyei, Z. (2005) *The Psychology of the Language Learner: Individual Differences in Second Language Acquisition*, Mahwah, NJ: Lawrence Erlbaum.

Dörnyei, Z. and Ushida, E. (2001) *Teaching and Researching Motivation*, London: Longman.

## Aneta Pavlenko

Aneta Pavlenko covers a wide range of topics in her research, including sociocultural theory, narrative research, cross-cultural aspects of emotions, psycholinguistics and identity. Recently, she started working on the linguistic landscape, in particular with respect to the study of Russian abroad.

"The scope of her research is very wide, but that doesn't mean that the way she does research is shallow." "Links many subfields in a deep way."

President of AAAL 2015.

Pavlenko, A. and Blackledge, A. (eds) (2004) *Negotiation of Identities in Multilingual Contexts*, Clevedon: Multilingual Matters.

Pavlenko, A. and Lantolf, J. (2000) "Second language learning as participation and the (re)construction of selves" in: J. Lantolf (ed.), *Sociocultural Theory and Second Language Learning*, Oxford: Oxford University Press, pp. 155–77.

## John Schumann

John Schumann has worked on affect and SLA, pidginization, acculturation, complex adaptive systems, and the foundations of language development. He has also published on the neurobiology of affect and language development.

"He is a free-thinking spirit that has had impact through his work on acculturation, emotions and 'the interactional instinct'." "The only applied linguist who crosses the bridge to the neurobiology of language and a strong believer in complex adaptive systems as a model for language and language learning." "Well known for his colored bowties."

Schumann, J. (1978) *The Pidginization Process: A Model for Second Language Acquisition*, Rowley, MA: Newbury House.

Schumann, J. (1986) "Research on the acculturation model for second language acquisition", *Journal of Multilingual and Multicultural Development*, vol. 7, no. 5: 379–92.

### G. Richard (Dick) Tucker

Dick Tucker worked with Wallace Lambert on the famous St Lambert project in Montreal. Later, he became the director of the Centre of Applied Linguistics (CAL) for a long time. His research covers language policy, immersion and bilingual education and individual differences in language learning.

"As the director of CAL he managed to stay above the parties in many of the fierce debates on language teaching during that time." "He has connected the field with relevant policy makers." "He is highly respected as a mentor for many researchers and students all over the world." "He is famous for his incredible knowledge of the field and applied linguists all over the world." "He and his collaborators helped to elucidate both social psychological richness of bilingualism and the feasibility of excellent L2 instruction through immersion programs." "Generous, totally weary of self-promotion, but important."

Lambert, W., Tucker, R. and d'Anglejan, A. (1973) "Cognitive and attitudinal consequences of bilingual schooling", *Journal of Educational Psychology*, vol. 65, no. 2: 141–56.

Tucker, G. Richard and Corson, D. (1997) *Second Language Education*, New York: Springer.

## 4.4 Conclusion

In this chapter the leadership in AL has been investigated. Leaders can define a field, for instance in the way Chomsky has done for linguistics as a field. It seems that in AL there are no leaders of that type. The informants listed the people they regarded as leaders in the field. Though a total of 228 names were mentioned with 58 names mentioned at least four times, there seems to be a consensus on who are the top leaders in our field. The leaders typically have a high academic standing, are innovative in their work and not focused on single issues in their careers. Most of them are also active in national and international AL associations, and act as editors of journals or book series.

Most of the leaders are based in North America. Non-American leaders are typically mentioned by non-American informants. Americans mention few non-Americans as leaders. A majority of the people mentioned as leaders are men, but in the top five there are three women.

Why are there no leaders of the Chomsky type in AL? Strong leaders tend to have strong views, and though the people listed as leaders clearly have their views, they tend to be open to other perspectives and opinions, and followers are free to think otherwise. There may be schools, but there are no religions in AL. This may be related to the fact that AL is largely an empirical discipline and that implies that beliefs have to be supported by convincing empirical evidence. *Ex cathedra* statements without such support are unlikely to gain power. Another factor may be that AL deals with so many subdisciplines, which all have their connections with other disciplines. The main authority for such a subdiscipline may not be at the core of AL but elsewhere, and that is where the leaders are, too.

# 5  Most important articles and books in AL

Communication in a discipline takes place mainly through books and journal articles. Themes develop through interactions in various forms of publication. We may assume that for each discipline there are publications that are seen as core by a significant proportion of the researchers involved. In this chapter, I want to look at the most important articles and books to see what that core is for AL as a discipline.

The two questions in the questionnaire were formulated as follows: "What are the 5–10 most important articles/book chapters for you over these 30 years?" and "What are the 5–10 most important books for you over these 30 years?"

Almost all informants complained that this is a very difficult task, and several of them gave up on this, mentioning "too many to list".

They also asked whether the publications should be the ones that were important for themselves or for the field as a whole. Interpretations differed; some informants clearly chose the publications that had been important for them, others listed publications that defined the field in their view. Since there is no objective way to find out what the informants had in mind while listing publications, it was decided to pull all the publications together.

Precision in referencing is not the most pronounced characteristic of my informants. Many left articles underspecified with respect to volume or pages, or even wrong information. For instance, Bley-Vroman's article in *Language Learning* was mentioned four times, but each time with a different year of publication (1981, 1982, 1983 and 1984). Similarly, the Firth and Wagner article in *The Modern Language Journal* was reported as published in a range of years.

## 5.1 Most important articles

The informants mentioned a staggering total of 424 articles with 111 duplicates, leaving a total of 313 unique articles. Of these, 131 articles are mentioned only once. A total of 106 applied linguists listed only two articles 11 times and two nine times and the rest seven times or less. This is remarkable given the selection of informants that represent only a part of what might be the field of AL.

The journals mentioned were: *Applied Linguistics* (AL), *The International Review of Applied Linguistics* (IRAL), *Language Learning* (LL), *The Modern Language Journal* (MLJ), *Studies in Second Language Acquisition* (SSLA) and *TESOL Quarterly* (TQ).

The following articles have been mentioned four times or more, with the number of listings in brackets:

Canale, M. and Swain, M. (1980) "Theoretical bases of communicative approaches to second language teaching and testing", *Applied Linguistics*, vol. 1, no. 1: 1–47. (11)

Firth, A. and Wagner, J. (1997) "On discourse, communication, and (some) fundamental concepts in SLA research", *The Modern Language Journal*, vol. 81, no. 3: 285–300. (11)

Norris, J. and Ortega, L. (2000) "Effectiveness of L2 instruction: A research synthesis and quantitative meta-analysis", *Language Learning*, vol. 50, no. 3: 417–528. (9)

Selinker, L. (1972) "Interlanguage", *International Review of Applied Linguistics in Language Teaching*, vol. 10, no. 1–4: 209–32. (9)

Larsen-Freeman, D. (1997) "Chaos/complexity science and second language acquisition", *Applied Linguistics*, vol. 18, no. 2: 141–65. (7)

Ellis, N.C. (1998) "Emergentism, connectionism and language learning", *Language Learning*, vol. 48, no. 4: 631–64. (6)

Meisel, J.M., Clahsen, H. and Pienemann, M. (1981) "On determining developmental stages in natural second language acquisition", *Studies in Second Language Acquisition*, vol. 3, no. 2: 109–35. (5)

The "Five Graces Group", Beckner, C., Blythe, R., Bybee, J., Christiansen, M.H., Croft, W., Ellis, N.C., Holland, J., Ke, J., Larsen-Freeman, D. and Schoenemann, T. (2009) "Language is a complex adaptive system: Position paper", *Language Learning*, vol. 59: 1–26. (5)

Cook, V. (1999) "Going beyond the native speaker in language teaching", *TESOL Quarterly*, vol. 33, no. 2: 185–209. (4)

Corder, S.P. (1967) "The significance of learner's errors", *International Review of Applied Linguistics in Language Teaching*, vol. 5, no. 1–4: 161–70. (4)

Gregg, K. (1984) "Krashen's monitor and Occam's razor", *Applied Linguistics*, vol. 5, no. 2: 79–100. (4)

Long, M. (1983) "Does second language instruction make a difference? A review of research", *TESOL Quarterly*, vol. 17, no. 3: 359–82. (4)

Schmidt, R.W. (1983) "Interaction, acculturation and the acquisition of communicative competence" in: N. Wolfson and E. Judd (eds), *Sociolinguistics and Language Acquisition*, Rowley, MA: Newbury House, pp. 137–74. (4)

Schmidt, R.W. (1990) "The role of consciousness in second language learning", *Applied Linguistics*, vol. 11, no. 2: 129–58. (4)

In this section informants listed both journal articles and book chapters. There are 77 book chapters, so the majority of the publications are journal articles. The oldest publication was Mitchell, T.F. (1954) "The language of buying and selling in Cyrenaica", *Hespéris*, vol. 44: 31–71, mentioned by Richard Young. The most recent is Aronin, L. (2014) "The concept of affordances in applied linguistics and multilingualism" in: M. Pawlak and L. Aronin (eds), *Essential Topics in Applied Linguistics and Multilingualism*, Heidelberg: Springer, pp. 157–73, mentioned by David Singleton. In fact, for more recent publications it is difficult to say whether they will become one of the most important ones, as for these publications the impact and importance still has to materialize.

There is no clear pattern in the topics the articles deal with, apart from the psycholinguistically oriented articles in the early 1980s and the first attempts to broaden the scope later on. It would be interesting to analyze the citation history of some of these key publications. The program HistCite (www.gar field.library.upenn.edu/histcomp/) would be suitable for this, but it turns out that this program is based on the information in Web of Science, an online platform that is strongly biased toward the hard sciences and medicine and does not sufficiently cover the humanities to get a good picture (see also Chapter 9 on this issue).

If we look at the journals in which the articles have been published, we see that there is a core of journals that are preferred. Table 5.1 lists the journals with the number of listings.

Although the list of the top journals is in line with the journals that are read regularly by the informants there is a remarkable gap here between *AL* and the other journals. This can be partly explained by the high frequency of the Canale and Swain article from 1980, although other journals also have

*Table 5.1* AL journals with the number of listings (>2)

| | |
|---|---|
| *Applied Linguistics* | 57 |
| *Studies in Second Language Acquisition* | 31 |
| *Language Learning* | 29 |
| *TESOL Quarterly* | 26 |
| *The Modern Language Journal* | 17 |
| *Second Language Research* | 17 |
| *IRAL* | 14 |
| *Journal of Social Issues* | 4 |
| *English Language Teaching Journal* | 4 |
| *Language* | 4 |
| *Review of Educational Research* | 4 |
| *International Journal of Applied Linguistics* | 3 |
| *Journal of Child Language* | 3 |
| *Psychological Review* | 3 |
| *Reading Research Quarterly* | 3 |
| *Applied Psycholinguistics* | 3 |
| *Bilingualism: Language and Cognition* | 3 |

articles that are mentioned often, such as Selinker in *IRAL*, Firth and Wagner in *MLJ* and Norris and Ortega in *LL*. It may have to do with the image of the journals, with *SSLA* and *LL* being seen as hardcore psycholinguistic journals, *TQ* as focusing on English teaching primarily and *MLJ* as more policy oriented. That leaves *AL* for a wide range of topics, also for those not primarily related to second or foreign languages. There may also be differences in the number of pages per year, but for the selection presented here that will not play a role.

In addition to the core AL journals, 15 more different journals are mentioned that are more peripheral to AL. This reflects once more the multidisciplinarity of the field.

For Jodi Crandall, book chapters are more important than journal articles to represent the stream of thinking. Maybe on the basis of that she also mentions that she recently threw away all of her printed journals (apart from the *Annual Review of Applied Linguistics!*), because they are now all available online.

## 5.2 Most important books

As with the journal articles, the range of books mentioned was impressive. A total of 478 books are listed, with 196 appearing only once. Books that have seen a number of editions over time, like Ellis's *The Study of SLA* and Spada and Lightbown's *How Languages are Learned*, have been listed as one entry. The books that have been mentioned at least three times with the total number of listings between brackets are:

Widdowson, H.G. (1990) *Aspects of Language Teaching*, Oxford: Oxford University Press. (8)

Krashen, S. (1982) *Principles and Practice in Second Language Acquisition*, Oxford: Pergamon. (7)

Ellis, R. (1986) *Understanding Second Language Acquisition*, Oxford: Oxford University Press. (7)

Ellis, R. (1994) *The Study of Second Language Acquisition*, Oxford: Oxford University Press. (6)

Lantolf, J.P. and Thorne, S.L. (2006) *Sociocultural Theory and the Genesis of Second Language Development*, Oxford: Oxford University Press. (6)

Tomasello, M. (2003) *Constructing a Language: A Usage-based Theory of Language Acquisition*, Cambridge, MA: Harvard University Press. (6)

Dörnyei, Z. (2005) *The Psychology of the Language Learner: Individual Differences in Second Language Acquisition*, Mahwah, NJ: Lawrence Erlbaum. (5)

Lantolf, J.P. (ed.) (2000) *Sociocultural Theory and Second Language Learning*, Oxford: Oxford University Press. (5)

Brice-Heath, S. (1983) *Ways with Words: Language, Life, and Work in Communities and Classrooms*, Cambridge: Cambridge University Press. (4)

Chaudron, C. (1988) *Second Language Classrooms: Research on Teaching and Learning*, Cambridge: Cambridge University Press. (4)

Doughty, C. and Long, M. (eds) (2003) *Handbook of Second Language Acquisition*, New York: Basil Blackwell. (4)

Gass, S. and Selinker, L. (1983) *Language Transfer in Language Learning*, Rowley, MA: Newbury House. (4)

Grosjean, F. (1982) *Life With Two Languages: An Introduction to Bilingualism*, Cambridge, MA: Harvard University Press. (4)

Gumperz, J. (1982) *Discourse Strategies*, Cambridge: Cambridge University Press. (4)

Hatch, E.M. (1978) *Second Language Acquisition: A Book of Readings*, Rowley, MA: Newbury House Publishers. (4)

Kachru, B. (1992) *The Other Tongue: English across Cultures*, Champaign: University of Illinois Press. (4)

Krashen, S.D. (1985) *The Input Hypothesis: Issues and Implications*, New York: Longman. (4)

Larsen-Freeman, D. and Cameron, L. (2008) *Complex Systems and Applied Linguistics*, Oxford: Oxford University Press. (4)

Larsen-Freeman, D. and Long, M.H. (1991) *An Introduction to Second Language Acquisition Research*, New York: Longman. (4)

Lightbown, P. and Spada, N. (1993) *How Languages are Learned*, Oxford: Oxford University Press. (4)

Pavlenko, A. (2005) *Emotions and Multilingualism*, Cambridge: Cambridge University Press. (4)

Skehan, P. (1998) *A Cognitive Approach to Language Learning*, Oxford: Oxford University Press. (4)

Van Lier, L. (1996) *Interaction in the Language Curriculum: Awareness, Autonomy and Authenticity*, London: Longman. (4)

Vygotsky, L.S. (1978) *Mind in Society: The Development of Higher Psychological Processes*, Cambridge, MA: Harvard University Press. (4)

White, L. (1989) *Universal Grammar and Second Language Acquisition*, Amsterdam and Philadelphia: John Benjamins Publishing. (4)

Some of the early books, like those by Allan, Corder and van Els *et al.* have vanished from sight, though to my great joy Robert Dekeyser mentioned the van Els *et al.* book: "Het boek waarvan ik het meest over toegepaste linguistiek heb geleerd is het *Handboek voor de Toegepaste Taalkunde* [the book from which I learned most about AL is the *Handbook for Applied Linguistics* by Theo van Els, Guus Extra, Charles van Os and Anne-Mieke Janssen-van Dieten (1977), later in 1984 translated and published by Edward Arnold]." "There was no other equally broad and thorough overview at that time", as Andrew Cohen remarked when he also mentioned this book by van Els *et al.*

Apart from Dante's *Divina Comédia*, written in the first half of the fourteenth century, the oldest book, mentioned by Hannele Dufva, was Valentin Voloshinov's *Marxism and the Philosophy of Language* (originally published in 1929, and in 1973 published in English by Harvard University Press). The most recent is Granena, G. and Long, M. (2014) *Sensitive Periods, Language*

*Aptitude and Ultimate L2 Attainment*, Amsterdam: John Benjamins Publishing, mentioned by Rod Ellis. The books are spread over time, with more books from the 1980s compared to other decades. Again, publications from 2000 onwards still need to develop their impact. As we will see in Chapter 9, many publications take 15 years to reach their highest impact.

## 5.3 The role of publishers

The publishing landscape has changed considerably over the last decades. There has been a complex process of merging publishing houses into larger conglomerates. For example, Edward Arnold had been publishing books for over 100 years when in 2001 it became part of Hodder Education, which in turn was sold to Taylor & Francis in 2012. In the 1980s, Newbury House was an important player, along with Prentice Hall, Erlbaum, Edward Arnold and the university presses (Cambridge and Oxford). Newbury House was taken over by Heinle, Prentice Hall focused on textbooks and Erlbaum seems to have stopped publishing books on AL. Routledge became one of the larger publishers in the field, but also two specialized publishers, John Benjamins and Multilingual Matters, became increasingly important. Their dedication and willingness to publish books for a fairly small market has led to an increase in status. While a couple of years ago the university presses had higher status, now the two specialized publishers are seen as equal, and most of the leading authors in the field have published books with them. The number of books they have produced is impressive and has grown almost linearly over the last 30 years. Figure 5.1 presents the number of books published on AL as defined in this study between 1980 and 2015 in five-year periods. A broader definition of AL would yield larger numbers, but the trend would probably remain the same.

The graphs show the enormous growth over time, at least for these two publishers. No information on the total volume of books published by all publishers is available, which makes the interpretation of Figure 5.1 problematic. It may be that John Benjamins and Multilingual Matters filled in the gap left by the discontinuation of publishers like Newbury House. These figures also support the earlier mentioned notion that books still count in our field, both as a means of communicating new ideas, and as a factor in promotion and hiring of new staff. Though in many countries peer-reviewed international journals are the main goal, a CV of an established applied linguist without one or more books is hard to imagine. As with the journals, there does not seem to be a tendency to publish books online only. A recent trend is that book chapters are becoming accessible electronically, which is particularly important for edited volumes. While books are underrepresented in databases like Web of Science and Google Scholar, book chapters that are available separately are typically more accessible than whole books. It should also be mentioned that the publishers are important sponsors for various AL related activities.

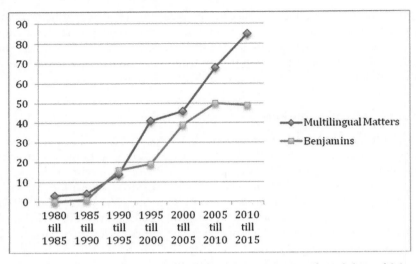

*Figure 5.1* Number of books published by John Benjamins and Multilingual Matters between 1980 and 2015

It could be argued that by setting up new book series and journals publishers define the field to a considerable extent. In this way, they also create a community of authors, editors and reviewers that more or less constitute the field.

## 5.4 Conclusion

This chapter presents the most important books and journals as listed by the informants. There is agreement on what the most important journals in the field are and these are mentioned more often than other journals that are either more peripheral or too recent to have had an impact.

For both journal articles and books a very large number of publications was mentioned with only a few of these being mentioned by a substantial number of informants. This suggests that even for the biased population in my study, which are basically the researchers working in the area of SLA, there is not really a common core of publications that defines the field and that every student of AL should read. The wide range of journals and books on the one hand reflects the interdisciplinarity of the field. On the other hand, it suggests that the cohesion of the field is fairly limited. In addition to the wide range of interpretations of what AL is, as discussed in Chapter 3, the data on the most important journal articles and books suggest that AL as a field is at best loosely structured. It would be useful to have similar data from other fields that are more tightly structured based on other criteria than the range of publications. Only then, conclusions can be drawn on the comparative looseness or tightness of AL as a field. In a way, the publishers may have been more influential in defining the field than the researchers and the literature they cite.

# 6 Main trends I
## Theoretical and methodological aspects

In this chapter and the following one, the responses to the question "What are the main trends over the last 30 years?" are presented. The complete list of topics mentioned is long and varied. I have attempted to bring topics together to make it more coherent, but the responses could have been structured in many different ways. Not all informants who mentioned certain trends are mentioned all the time. In some cases I have taken notions from various informants and combined them. The trends are structured into three sets. In this chapter the focus is on theoretical and methodological aspects of AL and in the next chapters topics related to psycholinguistics, sociolinguistics and education are presented. Chapter 8 discusses the dynamic turn.

## 6.1 Theoretical aspects

### 6.1.1 Linguistic theories

The last three decades have seen a proliferation of linguistic theories that have played a role in AL. Three theories have dominated the scene, though not all to the same degree or at the same time: Chomsky's Generative Grammar (GG), Usage based (UB) approaches with cognitive linguistics as its main component and Halliday's Systemic Functional Grammar (SFG). This section assumes some knowledge about current linguistic theories and how they are applied to language learning. A detailed description of the various theories is beyond the scope of this book.

To start with the latter, this theory is based on "meaning potential", as for Halliday linguistics is the study of "how people exchange meaning by 'languaging'" (1985: 193). Grammar is functional "since language has evolved in the process of carrying out certain functions as human beings interacted with their 'eco-social' environment" (2013: 1). While SFG has a very strong position in Australia, its impact in other parts of the world seems to be fairly limited, though it is the leading theory on language in a number of universities, in particular Georgetown, where Heidi Byrnes managed to reform the German program according to the principles of SFG, but also Berkeley and Birmingham. Few of the informants refer to SFG as a linguistic theory that can cover the roles, forms and functions of language and language use, even though that is exactly what its proponents claim. The SFG community seems to be inward looking and inbreeding, with its own conferences and symposia at conferences like AAAL. The complexity of the formalisms is seen as a prohibitive factor in adopting this perspective. It is generally acknowledged that SFG was focusing on meaning, relevance and applicability in different walks of life well before other UB approaches emerged. It is a forerunner in the "eco-linguistics" trend. SFG has not been in competition with other theories the way GG and UB approaches have. It is as if the SFG linguists and the GG linguists have been living in different realms, just like having their own worlds that do not seem to overlap.

On the basis of comments made by the informants, a spectacular growth of SFG in AL is not expected, though Tim McNamara feels that the United States is ready for SFG. William Grabe disagrees: "SFG is not the solution. There is not enough empirical evidence. The theory is arcane, the terminology complex and the texts are often painful to read." When asked why Halliday never took off in the United States, he remarked jokingly: "Because he moved to Australia!"

GG has been the dominant theory for most of the decades covered in this book. One of the most important representatives of this approach is Lydia White, who sees "development of generative linguistic approaches to SLA" as one of the major trends. Similar reactions come from various researchers from the GG community. María del Pilar García Mayo says: "I think the field of formal SLA, led by Roger Hawkins, Bonnie Schwartz and Lydia White has seen a tremendous growth in theoretical issues, type of data collected and methodologies used." Bill VanPatten is optimistic about what is happening with GG:

> I see growth, if you mean its use as a framework (and not how the actual framework itself has evolved). I think it's reached stasis though; that is, its use to investigate SLA has neither declined nor increased recently as I see it. What we have seen, at the same time, is an increase in other frameworks – this is perhaps giving some people the idea that the research from a GG perspective has declined. But it hasn't.

According to Camilla Bardel L3 research from a GG perspective has added new air to the research field by reopening old discussions with fresh data.

But there are also other views. Joan Kelly Hall noticed a move away from mainstream psychology and formal linguistics. Alan Juffs sees as one of the major trends: "The rise, then fall of a role for formal linguistics, and the rise of connectionist approaches." Wolfgang Klein refers to "attempts to apply generative grammar, in particular the notion of parameter setting, to language acquisition."

GG is generally seen as a declining paradigm and its proponents now tend to stay away from conferences like AAAL (the American Association of

Applied Linguistics) and University of Boston Child Language Development conferences, as a cursory count of papers on the basis of abstracts shows. Suzanne Flynn, one of the early adapters of GG to SLA, is "disappointed with the way things have turned out". She also refers to the factions that developed within the GG community and the competition and rivalry that have harmed the enterprise. There is "dancing on Chomsky's grave" and Chomsky-bashing rather than an evaluation of what parts of the theory are relevant for AL. She regrets the – in her view unhealthy – competition in the GG community, "your religion – my religion," rather than data driven. She decided to move to research on dementia and L3 rather than core GG/SLA.

For Andrea Tyler the decline of GG went further than the abandoning of a paradigm: "The current big gap between linguistics generally and language teaching was partly caused by the fact that GG could not explain many aspects of SLA and many people gave up linguistics due to the GG failure." Rod Ellis mentions that in the forthcoming edition of his *Understanding SLA* there will no longer be a separate chapter on GG-based approaches to SLA, but only some paragraphs in the chapter on linguistic approaches.

Jim Lantolf regrets that there is no real discussion between camps or openness for each other's arguments:

> We both can't be right. But who is willing to invest the time to really understand the other theory. How to reach a synthesis? I do follow developments in UG, but the UG people don't have time, there are isolated camps with different cultures. Is there progress if we only develop in our own community or way of thinking?

While for the language as a social phenomenon community the GG research and the psycholinguistic community are seen as one group with the overall label "cognitive", there have been serious controversies between these two communities. In my view, it is no coincidence that in Levelt's (1989) ground-breaking book on language production there is only one reference to Chomsky, and that is not N. but C. Chomsky. In the psycho-linguistic community, the idea of innateness and a Language Acquisition Device (LAD) were seen as problematic, and the leading institute in the world, the Max Planck Institute for Psycholinguistics in Nijmegen was ostensibly anti-GG. This is also reflected in Levelt's early criticism of the GG model in his 1975 work *What Happened to LAD?*

There is also a sociological component in the debate about the position of GG at universities. Starting from the 1960s, GG was seen as the new way to go and many linguistics departments turned Chomskian, which led to se-rious conflicts with linguists of other persuasions who felt sidetracked. Now that generation of GG linguists is retiring and there is a tendency in many universities not to replace them with younger scholars of that school, but rather appoint UB oriented linguists. There is almost a euphoria that the grip of the nativists on what constitutes linguistics is gone and that other approaches and more social orientations are seen as meaningful alternatives. Others try to explain the reasons for the decline of GG. Michael Sharwood Smith comments:

> A distinct decline in interest within AL in general when it took a more (generative) linguistic character, partly due to its highly technical nature plus the insistence of mainstream SLA researchers (at the time) that their focus was not on language teaching so, for many people, GG simply decisively confirmed the new border between SLA narrowly defined and AL although this did not prevent any researcher, like VanPatten for example, from having a foot in both camps.

Some informants are quite outspoken about the role of GG in AL. William Grabe states: "Fundamentally Chomsky is wrong and we wasted a lot of time. In 1964 Chomsky's *Aspects* was published. Now, in 2014, we are 50 years later. What impact has all of that had in real world language use? This is an overstated theoretical direction." Jan Hulstijn summarizes: "Generative linguistics has had no noticeable (or durable) impact."

The growth of more usage based (UB) approaches is partly a reaction to both the GG people and the neo-behaviorist psycholinguists. The core idea of approaches that are referred to as UB is that grammar is not innate, as GG assumes, and that language development results from the interaction of general purpose cognitive mechanisms and a rich linguistic environment. Michael Tomasello is often referred to as the leading figure in the UB movement. For the application of UB to SLA, Nick Ellis and Andrea Tyler are mentioned as playing an important role. UB means that learning is primarily statistical learning and that patterns of use emerge through interaction and input. No rules are assumed, though views on that vary. The distinction between what constitutes a rule and what is a pattern is less than clear.

Cognitive linguistics emerged in the 1970s from research on concepts underlying forms. There are now cognitive approaches to semantics, grammar and phonology. Language learning is based on input mainly, and language is seen as a social phenomenon. Cognitive linguistics is seen as a useful contribution to the application of Socio-Cultural Theory (SCT) to SLA. The growth of SCT is one of the most frequently mentioned main trends. The problem with the Vygotskian approach is that it is a theory of development, but not specifically of language. The assumptions behind cognitive linguistics are seen as a useful addition to fill that gap. Chuming Wang sees the growth of UB approaches as a positive development:

> The emergence of educational linguistics, which strikes me as a sub-branch of AL, makes a more focused study of language teaching possible. The more recent development of the UB approach to SLA, it seems to me, bears more on language teaching than any other approaches, although more research along this line is called for before the potential of this approach for language education can be fully tapped.

Several informants mention the lack of linguistic sophistication in recent AL research. Martin Bygate says:

> A final trend is the absence of much (sometimes of any) sophisticated linguistics in AL research. The time it has taken for people to start critiquing and refining the measures used in the CAF (complexity/accuracy/fluency) studies is an example of this. Similarly, the lack of any sustained critique of the shallow linguistics used in the early acquisition order studies.

His views are endorsed by Kathleen Bardovi-Harlig: "There is less linguistics as the years go by. Applied linguists are less well trained. There are more and more programs with none of the core linguistic areas."

### 6.1.2 *Theory construction and Second Language Acquisition (SLA)*

Jordan's book *Theory Construction in Second Language Acquisition* (2004) reflects a need in the field to develop theories of relevant aspects of AL. This can be seen in the special issue of the journal *Applied Linguistics* on theory construction in SSLA (1993). Michael Long (1993) estimates that there are between 40 and 60 theories of SLA. Jim Lantolf, in his famous "Letting all the flowers bloom" article in *Language Learning* from 1996, pleads for the allowance of as many theories as needed, but in the interview he took a different position and argued that just as science tries to come up with one big theory about the universe, AL should also aim at the construction of such an encompassing theory. Many informants feel that there is no need for one overarching theory, since the field consists of many subfields with their own theories.

For Alister Cumming what is important for the field is "recognition of the complex, variable, and multi-faceted dimensions of language learning and of education rather than any preferred, singular teaching method or uniform progression of SLA". This is also mentioned by Lourdes Ortega, who argues that "the big question we want to answer is: Why is the learning of an additional language such a complex task?" But she also warns that "to date we may have focused too much on asking why is it so difficult for adults to learn a second language, why is L2 learning so different from anything else?" In her opinion, "these framings of complexity are negative and dangerous, because they can unwittingly perpetuate a deficiency view of multilingualism and encourage disciplinary isolationism".

### 6.1.3 *The relativist/rationalist debate*

The fundamental debate between relativists and rationalists is probably one of the fiercest in the last decades. Jordan's book and reactions to it (Thomas 2005; Gregg 2005) have sparked that debate and as Jim Lantolf remarked: "I still have scars from that." A complete treatment of this debate and its philosophical background is beyond the scope of the present book. The relativist position, defended by people like Block, Lantolf, Firth and Wagner, is that there are multiple realities and that phenomena are always contextualized and contingent on other phenomena. The rationalist position, defended by people like Crookes, Eubank, Gregg and Long, state that there is one reality that we can observe objectively without the researcher influencing the data.

The debate continues. Michael Long takes a clear position when asked about the main trends: "Appearance of relativist work by a small but vocal minority, with some inevitable damage done to the credibility of SLA and AL as a result. Hopefully, this will be a passing phase, as it has been in other disciplines." His views are not shared by all informants. Many of them see a growth of research with a relativist perspective and a substantial development of the SCT community.

Jan Hulstijn refers to the gap between the quantitative and qualitative approach to research:

> The gap between, on the one side, researchers investigating linguistic-cognitive issues, often using quantitative research methods including inferential statistics and, on the other side, researchers working on the basis of sociocultural or sociocognitive views, often using qualitative research methods, including case study and ethnography. The gap was perhaps more apparent in the 1990s than presently.

But Merrill Swain still wonders: "What are the standards for qualitative research? There are standards, but often they are not adhered to." This gap is discussed in the nine-author article (Hulstijn *et al.* 2014) in SSLA.

As Nunan (1992) indicates, the debate is ultimately philosophical:

> One reason for the persistence of the distinction between quantitative and qualitative research is that the two approaches represent different ways of thinking about and understanding the world around us. Underlying the development of different research traditions and methods is a debate on the nature of knowledge and the status of assertions about the world, and the debate itself is ultimately a philosophical one ... Underpinning quantitative research is the positivistic notion that the basic function of research is to uncover facts and truths which are independent of the researcher. Qualitative researchers question the notion of an objective reality.

(10)

### 6.1.4 The growth of Socio-Cultural Theory

Many informants see the emergence and growth of SCT as one of the most important trends. While SCT was marginal for many years, it has gained substantial popularity in the last decade.

As mentioned earlier, the problem with the Vygotskian approach is that it is a theory of development, but not specifically of language. Cognitive linguistics is seen as a useful contribution to the application of SCT to SLA, since it provides a theory of what constitutes language that is in line with some of the core assumptions in SCT.

Why SCT caught on so massively is not clear. According to Tim McNamara, Merrill Swain's move into SCT provided it with more credibility, and made it "salonfähig" (socially acceptable). Jim Lantolf assumes that the mentioning of SCT as a theory for AL in handbooks and overviews like Ellis (1994) and Mitchell *et al.* (2013) is the main factor. Also the AL community seemed to be ready to accept a more socially based theory as a reaction to the dominant psycholinguistic approaches in the 1970s and 1980s.

William Grabe relates the growth of SCT with the development of what might be called SCT-Light. An SCT analysis can be done very rigorously "but sometimes it can be done very superficially". In his view, it is much easier to do a SCT-Light analysis of classroom interaction than to set up a complicated experiment with human subjects. He feels that SCT needs to be based on empirical research; introspection is not enough. Of course, this raises the question of what counts as empirical data. For some this implies quantification and statistics, while others see introspective data, stimulated recalls and think aloud protocols as equally valid.

### 6.1.5 Foundational sources and reinventing the wheel

Many informants argue for more attention for the foundational literature of the field. Albert Weideman in particular stresses the need to link developments in the field with essential foundational concepts. The basis of what is now seen as AL was laid in the 1970s and 1980s by people like Corder, Hymes, Labov, Grice, Fishman and Halliday, and even further back by Wundt and de Saussure. That is not to say that reading such classics is easy. Karen Johnson remembers that, in a course, she had to read Vygotsky in original form "and we had no clue what we were reading". Many of the things these eminent researchers said are still relevant and students of AL should be made aware of that. But that literature should also be framed or reinterpreted in the light of what happened after that. The old literature should, in my view, not be like a gospel, but awareness of the ideas expressed in them is useful. We also need conveyers and interpreters of these traditions. The obvious example in AL is the growth of interest in SCT. Without the reinterpretation by people like Lantolf, Thorne and van Lier of the original writings by Vygotsky and other researchers in that tradition, the interest in it would certainly not have been what it is now.

Henry Widdowson (2003) points to the tendency to recycle old ideas without recognizing that they are old and the failure to take advantage of previous thinking. He further says:

On the one hand, it is irksome to find old ideas appearing in new packaging without knowledge, or acknowledgement, of their origins, and the discussion of issues in ignorance or disregard of how they have been dealt with in the past. But on reflection, this process of rediscovery seems entirely natural and desirable ... The very fact that ideas and issues, no matter how old their provenance, are taken up again makes them new, gives them a recharged vitality; and every new generation needs to think afresh for itself, appropriate the past and make it demonstrably their own.

(xi)

He concludes by citing L.P. Hartley: "The past is another country; they do things differently there."

A similar worry is expressed by Annick De Houwer: "Unfortunately, one trend has also been the forgetting or ignoring what has already been studied! So a lot of re-inventing the wheel and a basic lack of historical perspective."

### 6.1.6 *Definition of concepts*

Both Martin Bygate and Rod Ellis comment on the lack of clarity in defining concepts. Martin Bygate:

It is quite common for concepts to be poorly defined. The cognition hypothesis has invoked the "here & now/there & then" distinction, the former ("here and now") supposedly easier in tasks than the latter ... Yet even where both interlocutors can see the same data, it cannot be assumed that the mapping of language to referent is unproblematic. Yet in spite of this, dozens of papers continue to appear using this construct, none of them as far as I can see concerned with questioning the tools that they are using.

Rod Ellis sees as a major trend the exponential growth of labels to define key concepts in new theories:

We are constantly introducing new terms to label concepts that may or may not be new, but don't spend enough time carefully defining our constructs. There are too many vaguely defined concepts. If we want to communicate with each other, we need carefully defined concepts.

One of the examples that he mentions is the label "languaging".

## 6.2 Research methodology

### 6.2.1 *Research methods*

The range of research methods that is used in different types of AL research has grown considerably in the last decades. Most of these methods were imported from other disciplines like sociology, anthropology, psychology and neuroscience. They range from grammaticality judgments to think aloud protocols and very detailed conversational analysis techniques, surveys and various neuro-imaging techniques. Multi-method approaches are becoming popular, such as neuro-imaging combined with eye movement registration, or variation analysis and reaction time data. As Merrill Swain indicates, along with the increased sophistication of the methods comes a growth in the number and quality of statistical procedures. While in the 1980s knowledge of analysis of variance and correlations was enough, now more advanced techniques are becoming increasingly popular. Multilevel analysis, time series analysis, log-linear modeling and *Monte Carlo* iterations can now be found in many more recent publications. Peter Robinson says:

> You look at the early empirical work on language learning and effects of instruction (say Seliger and Long, 1983), and compare it to today (e.g., Gass and Mackey, 2012), and there has just been so much growth and sophistication in research methods and tools, and interdisciplinary links to both ... That is a major development.

### 6.2.2 The impact of corpus linguistics

One of the major trends has been the development of corpus linguistics. The enormous growth of corpus linguistics inspired by John Sinclair and his colleagues has made massive data available. The corpora are based on real authentic language use and that has led to a claim that all language teaching materials should be based on such authentic language. But as Henry Widdowson has argued in various publications, what is relevant and authentic for a native speaker in a specific situation is not necessarily relevant for a learner who is in a totally different situation:

> The claim of pedagogical relevance was based on the assumption that the language used in classrooms to induce the learning process had to be real or authentic use of native speakers as recorded in the corpus ... What came from a corpus, it was claimed, carried the guarantee of real language and therefore of pedagogical relevance. I objected that one could not assume that what was real for users was also real for learners since what made the language real was not its occurrence as text but its use as discourse and this crucially depended on contextual factors that the corpus did not record and the classroom could not replicate.
>
> (2009: xxv)

The other problem resulting from the growth of corpus linguistics is that the accessibility of data has led to a substantial growth of language description at the expense of theorizing. It is all very well to describe the use of language in services in churches in South Alabama, but what does it all mean? As Barbara Seidlhofer puts it: "Digging deep in corpus data is easy, a BA student can do it because corpora are very accessible, but the reflection on those data is lacking. There needs to be a balance between description and theorizing."

For some informants, the main contribution of corpus linguistics is that it made real language visible and accessible for research. The corpus data are seen as largely incompatible with assumptions in the GG tradition that are based on the idealized native speaker. There is now a tendency to develop corpora for specific groups of language users, such as Grainger's language learners' corpora and the Vienna corpus of users of English as a lingua franca.

### 6.2.3 Discourse analysis and conversational analysis

The growth of interest in discourse analysis and conversational analysis is one of the breakthroughs in AL over this period. Mary McGroarty notices:

> expanded attention to discourse analysis of all sorts, conducted in many different contexts; some of this work uses discourse analytic techniques in the service of analyzing, e.g. legal documents and processes (for example, Roger Shuy's work in the US; Diana Eades' in Australia).

She interprets the growth of interest in pragmatics as a reaction to the almost exclusively syntactic/grammatical focus of the 1960s and 1970s. Her views are shared by Hannele Dufva who notices "a move from a very narrow, structuralist view of language as a formal system consisting of different levels (syntax to phonology) towards broader views, including pragmatics, discourse, interaction etc. and quite recently, towards understanding the essential multimodality of language use". Johannes Wagner mentions: "CA for SLA, the sociologically inspired subfield which is quite different from the research about the interaction hypothesis by Mike Long, Susan Gass and others." The methodology of CA is debated extensively. Its principled stance to stick with the text and the text only makes the findings problematic in many informants' views. Tim McNamara sees what counts as evidence in studies using CA as the main methodology as the main problem.

### 6.2.4 Critical approaches

There is a remarkable lack of references to various "critical" approaches, such as critical discourse analysis, and even critical applied linguistics. Alan Davies sees a "lengthy flirtation with critical approaches in AL". Albert Weideman remarks: "A post-modern analysis without political action is vacuous." Robert Phillipson concludes that: "There is a reluctance to be multi-disciplinary and more critical."

### 6.2.5 *Neurolinguistics and the neurobiology of language*

There has been a significant growth in the number of studies using various neuro-imaging techniques. Jean-Marc Dewaele sees as a trend: "The realization that neuro-imaging is fascinating but doesn't offer easy answers – only more questions on how to interpret the findings." According to Barbara Seidlhofer, "there is always the danger that approaches to language and multilingualism claim to be linked to neuroscience without being sufficiently well informed. This sometimes leads to claims being made that go well beyond the data". According to John Schumann the main aim of neuro-linguistics has been to show that there is a neural correlate of the language acquisition device in the brain. So the approach has been to present subjects with specific stimuli that represented certain linguistic phenomena or rules and see how specific parts of the brain show activity. The view on the brain is essentially modular: there are parts of the brain that are dedicated to certain tasks. Researchers in the neurobiology of language, of which John Schumann is likely to be the only one who would also call himself an AL, take another perspective: "The brain is degenerate, not modular. Through use, parts of the brain become functional, and areas can do various things and they are colonized and reused according to need." As he mentions, the entry fee to do proper research in the area of neurobiology is high, and it is not clear whether the investment is worthwhile. "The neurobiology of language isn't going to make a breakthrough in AL. On the other hand, do we really want a brainless AL?"

### 6.2.6 *The role of technology*

Technological developments made it possible to deal with big data, such as large corpora for corpus analysis. While in the 1980s working with corpora demanded advanced computer skills, new technological developments have made these corpora much easier to handle. According to Diane Larsen-Freeman:

> The impact of technology has been slower to come than expected, but it is growing. With technology, a different way of engaging with information can be envisioned, a more dynamic and nonlinear one. We also can appreciate the potential affordances of social media that learners can take advantage of and how they reduce distance among their contemporaries around the world. We need to know more about how the multitasking and computer use of the younger generation influence their learning. Then, too, technology has allowed us to compile and search databases for recurrent lexicogrammatical sequences with which to inform teaching materials.

For Ben Rampton globalization and new media "have changed the world around us, undermining conceptual frameworks built on 'methodological nationalism', and presenting a whole range of new communicative dynamics and processes". Similar views are expressed by Durk Gorter, who sees as a major trend: "The internet and technology and its consequences for interconnectedness, for using (and learning) languages, for publications, for research, or, in general, for how we do our work and live our life."

Another aspect of technology is the emergence of social media and their impact on communication and linguistic variation. This is a fairly recent development and the average age of the informants is such that they are not typically the forerunners in this respect, but the potential impact is generally seen as relevant.

There has been an enormous growth of what is generally labeled as Computer Assisted Language Learning (CALL). Though some people such as Joan Kelly Hall argue that the same type of meaningless exercises continue to be used, but now with a computer rather than a teacher, others feel that the new technologies have led to better teaching, e.g. through the role of corpora and online resources.

### 6.2.7 Ethics in testing

A number of informants talk about the issue of ethics in testing. Tim McNamara remembers that when Elana Shohamy first raised, in a provocative way, the political character of language testing (already raised by Bernard Spolsky, but more moderately), he at first rejected her argument and felt wounded by her attack, but now he realizes that the liberal approach to ethics in language testing as exemplified by the work of Alan Davies and Anthony Kunnan is inadequate.

### 6.2.8 Meta-analyses and overview studies

Alan Juffs comments on the role of meta-analyses, which he sees as an important new development since they could lead to conclusive results for specific controversial issues. The most (in)famous meta-analysis in our field is probably the Baker and De Kanter study from 1983 on the effectiveness of bilingual education. Their conclusion is that the studies available do not show a positive effect for bilingual education. Baker and De Kanter have been criticized on various aspects of the study, including the random assignment to conditions and the selection of studies in the meta-analysis. Willig (1985) re-analyzed the dataset of the Baker and De Kanter study and found a positive effect of the use of the children's mother tongue in education. This shows the complexity of meta-analyses: they may create the kind of problems they intend to solve. Even for meta-analyses, questions of selection of studies and their interpretation arise. The goal of most meta-analyses is to end a long discussion on specific problems and to integrate all research that meets certain criteria and adds to the knowledge about the problem. In the field of AL, the best-known example of a meta-analysis is

John Norris and Lourdes Ortega's study, which was published in *Language Learning* in 2000. This study is seen as one of the most important articles in our field in the last decades and several informants call for more such studies, but as Lourdes Ortega mentions, for many topics there are simply not enough good quality studies available. In fact, the criteria for inclusion in such meta-analyses may be guidelines for good research in AL. Rod Ellis sees a number of problems with meta-analysis. His main problem is the "apples and pears" problem: what exactly do you compare? Another problem is that "most meta-analyses are not based on articles that make a direct comparison of the contrasted approaches, but look at articles that do one or the other without a direct comparison". He also worries that people will only look at effect sizes without a proper analysis of how the study was done.

A related trend that we have seen is the large number of encyclopedias and handbooks that have come out. There are *Handbooks of Applied Linguistics* (Davies and Elder 2004; Kaplan 2010), *Second Language Acquisition* (Doughty and Long 2003), *Language Teaching* (Johnson and Johnson 1998) and *Bilingualism and Multilingualism* (Bhatia and Ritchie 2006). Though technically not meta-analyses, many of the articles in such handbooks present overviews of studies on certain topics and in that way shape AL. The downside is, as Alan Juffs noticed, that students, but also established researchers, will stick with such overviews and stop reading the older, but often more fundamental, studies in sufficient depth.

The growth of the number of handbooks and the success of the *Annual Review of Applied Linguistics* as a reference journal reflects the enormous growth of the number of publications in books and journals. This can also be seen in the catalogues of the main publishers in the field, John Benjamins, Multilingual Matters, Oxford University Press, Pearson and Routledge. John Benjamins is a good example. Since AILA (Association Internationale de Linguistique Appliquée) in Sydney in 1987, which marked their entrance in the field of AL, their list of books and journals on AL has grown steadily, as discussed in the previous chapter.

The need for handbooks and encyclopedias is probably a result of the proliferation of publications in science generally. This, in turn, is the result of the pressure to publish, which is now as common in the field of AL as in most other fields. AL tends to follow developments in the social sciences more than traditional humanities, though books still are important next to high-ranking journals. The handbooks provide overviews of research that otherwise would be more difficult to find and process.

### 6.2.9 Other research populations

New questions have come up through the study of new, or at any rate as yet unexplored, populations. Many informants point to Elaine Tarone's recent work with non-literate language learners as an important development. Some claim that generalizing over large populations without taking into account factors like literacy is becoming substandard in terms of research design. The whole language learning business is based on learning with written support, though some work on language learning with dyslexic learners also has looked at the reduction of the role of script and written support.

Fred Genesee sees a growing interest in K-12 and minority language learners. Both in North America and western Europe there is a tendency to do research on immersion settings that go beyond assessing that there are now negative effects. There is also more interest in the pedagogy of immersion and Content and Language Integrated Learning (CLIL). As he says: "Immersion is rich on research, CLIL is rich on pedagogy and they should be brought together." Lourdes Ortega argues that AL research has focused almost exclusively on elite bilingualism, college FL learning and hardly on minorities; this in contrast to what happens in Europe. She would like to see more groups in society able to profit from AL research, in particular linguistic minorities, heritage learners, but also for communication in hospitals and courts. Susan Gass agrees: "What do we know about non-elite multilingualism, the effects of migration?" At the same time Andrew Cohen argues that applied linguists should be concerned not only with incipient learners and basic skills but also with higher-level skills.

### 6.2.10  International comparisons

While for reading and math there are worldwide comparisons on how well students do, no such comparisons on the scale of, for example, TIMSS (Trends in International Mathematics and Science Study) and PIRLS (Progress in International Reading Literacy Studies) have been done for English or any other language. Lyle Bachman speculates why that is the case. In his view it would be technically possible to develop a test for making international comparisons in English and other languages, but the only proposal he is aware of for developing such a test for English failed because no one was willing to spend money on it.

### 6.2.11  Generalizability

Generalizability is the holy grail of empirical research. In fact, it is a dream in my view, because no study in our field can claim to be based on a sample that is representative of the population, since we do not know the parameters that define the population. Studying the typical second-year university students does not help either. John Schumann:

> Molenaar's work distinguishing ergodic research from idiographic inquiry that provides us with information that frees us from the notion that truth is found only in group studies. He shows that what is true for a group cannot be generalized to the individual except under very special conditions. Here we have a nice symmetry – traditional views have

argued that we cannot generalize from case studies to groups, and now we know we cannot generalize from groups to individuals.

## 6.3 Conclusion

This first list of trends shows that, in terms of theories and research methodology, the field has been and is moving. Some theories wane, others grow. There is a clear trend away from formal theoretical linguistics, in particular UG, to more socially oriented and usage based approaches. There is also a tendency to make the gap between psycholinguistic approaches and sociolinguistic approaches smaller. This is one of the results of the application of CDST, though that model still has to prove its worth.

The most important, but therefore not necessarily positively evaluated, developments are the decline of formal linguistics in AL, the growth of SCT and other theories that try to connect the psycho and the socio, the development of technology that made large scale corpus construction and analysis possible and the application of more advanced research techniques and statistics. In the last few decades we can also witness the growth of the range of research paradigms and techniques, ranging from conversational analysis to neurobiological methods. Again, this fanning out suggests that AL as a discipline is open to new developments in adjacent fields, both in terms of theories and in terms of research methods. More advanced statistical tools are being used, but at the same time the traditional views on generalizability based on sampling from a population are challenged. This adds to the complexity of the debate on qualitative and quantitative methods, since the boundaries between the two are blurring. Conversational analytic methods may be used to study dense data on language development using time series analysis. This is clearly a very recent development that is likely to have an impact in the future.

Several informants point out that the scientific rigor of AL research has improved dramatically, though standards for qualitative research that have been developed and tested are not always applied adequately. There is some concern about the fact that old ideas are presented without mentioning the original thoughts behind them, and therefore there is the risk of re-inventing the wheel, but that may also reflect the mean age of the group of informants in this study.

## References

Baker, K. and De Kanter, A. (1983) *Bilingual Education*, Lexington: Lexington Books.
Bhatia, T.K. and Ritchie, W.C. (eds) (2006) *The Handbook of Bilingualism*, Oxford: Blackwell.
Davies, A. and Elder, C. (2004) *The Handbook of Applied Linguistics*, Oxford: Blackwell.
Doughty, C. and Long, M. (eds) (2003) *The Handbook of Second Language Acquisition*, London: Blackwell.

Ellis, R. (1994) *The Study of Second Language Acquisition*, Oxford: Oxford University Press.

Gass, S. and Mackey, A. (eds) (2012) *The Routledge Handbook of Second Language Acquisition*, London: Routledge.

Gregg, K.R. (2005) "A response to Jordan's (2004) 'Explanatory Adequacy and Theories of Second Language Acquisition'", *Applied Linguistics*, vol. 26, no. 1: 121–4.

Halliday, M. (1985) "Systemic background" in: J.D. Benson and W.S. Greaves (eds) *Systemic Perspectives on Discourse, Vol. 1: Selected Theoretical Papers* from the *Ninth International Systemic Workshop*, vol. 3 in *The Collected Works*, p. 193.

Halliday, M. (2013) "Meaning as choice" in: L. Fontaine, T. Bartlett and W. O'Grady (eds) *Choice: Critical Considerations in Systemic Functional Linguistics*, Cambridge: Cambridge University Press, pp. 1–17.

Hulstijn, J.H., Young, R.F., Ortega, L., Bigelow, M., DeKeyser, R., Ellis, N.C., Lantolf, J.P., Mackey, A. and Talmy, S. (2014) "Bridging the gap: Cognitive and social approaches to research in second language learning and teaching", *Studies in Second Language Acquisition*, vol. 36, no. 3: 361–421.

Johnson, K. and Johnson, H. (eds) (1998) *The Encyclopedic Dictionary of Applied Linguistics: A Handbook for Language Teaching*, London: Wiley-Blackwell.

Jordan, G. (2004) *Theory Construction in Second Language Acquisition*, Amsterdam and Philadelphia: John Benjamins.

Kaplan, R. (ed.) (2010) *The Oxford Handbook of Applied Linguistics*, 2nd edn, Oxford: Oxford University Press.

Lantolf, J. (1996) "SLA theory building: 'Letting all the flowers bloom'", *Language Learning*, vol. 46: 713–49.

Larsen-Freeman, D. (1997) "Chaos/complexity science and second language acquisition", *Applied Linguistics*, vol. 18, no. 2: 141–65.

Levelt, W. (1975) *What Happened To LAD?* The Hague: Peter de Ridder Press.

Levelt, W.J.M. (1989) *Speaking: From Intention to Articulation*, Cambridge, MA: The MIT Press.

Long, M. (1993) "The assessment of SLA theories", *Applied Linguistics*, vol. 14, no. 3: 225–49.

Mitchell, R., Myles, F. and Marsden, E. (2013) *Second Language Learning Theories*, London: Routledge.

Norris, J. and Ortega, L. (2000) "Effectiveness of L2 instruction: A research synthesis and quantitative meta-analysis", *Language Learning*, vol. 50, no. 3: 417–528.

Nunan, D. (1992) *Research Methods in Language Learning*, Cambridge: Cambridge University Press.

Seliger, H. and Long, M. (eds) (1983) *Classroom Oriented Research in Second Language Acquisition*, Rowley, MA: Newbury House.

Thomas, M. (2005) "Theories of second language acquisition: Three sides, three angles, three points", *Second Language Research*, vol. 21, no. 4: 393–414.

Widdowson, H. (2003) "'Expert beyond experience': Notes on the appropriate use of theory in practice" in: D. Newby (ed.), *Mediating between Theory and Practice*, Graz: Council of Europe Publishing, pp. 23–30.

Widdowson, H. (2009) "Remembrance of things past" in: C. Candlin (ed.), *Selected Works of Henry Widdowson*, Beijing: Foreign Language Teaching and Research Press, pp. VII–XXXII.

Willig, A. (1985) "A meta-analysis of selected studies on the effectiveness of bilingual education", *Review of Educational Research*, vol. 55, no. 3: 269–317.

# 7 Trends II
## Psycholinguistic, sociolinguistic and educational aspects

For the topical organization of the trends mentioned in the previous chapter that do not deal with theories and research methodology, the traditional distinction between psycholinguistic, sociolinguistic and educational aspects has been used, even though over time the boundaries between these first two have become less clear.

## 7.1 Psycholinguistic aspects: language and cognition

The definition of psycholinguistics in AL is not clear. It seems to refer to all approaches that see language primarily as an individual's commodity residing in the brain. SLA research looks at how humans develop and use languages. In some theories the human learner is endowed with a special language acquisition device that is innate. Input triggers the language acquisition device and limits the set of possible patterns and rules. A core issue in this tradition is to what extent the innate capacities that play a role only in first language acquisition, also play a role in the acquisition of later learned languages. While this issue was hot in the 1990s, the issue seems to have petered out after that, with no empirical evidence to decide between the two options. In other theories no innateness is assumed, and language development results from the interaction of basic, non-linguistic cognitive skills with a rich linguistic environment.

### 7.1.1 The role of input, output and interaction

The role of input has become one of the main issues in AL. It was a prominent feature of the Krashen model, in particular in the form of comprehensible input. Because it turned out to be difficult to define comprehensible input, it lost importance, even more so when Swain started stressing the need for output on the basis of findings in Canadian immersion education. But input continues to be crucial for development. Stephen Krashen says: "Most important for me is that we no longer assume that we acquire languages by conscious learning and output practice. This was an axiom, but it has been demoted to the status of hypothesis." According to Robert

DeKeyser, input is seen as more important now than in the past. Elizabeth Lanza concurs:

> In the field of bilingual first language acquisition, psycholinguists have in recent years acknowledged the need to take into account the impact of input on bilingual language acquisition. This was previously a neglected aspect of study. However, what is currently in vogue is not a conception of input as interactional, that is, qualitative; rather, a quantifiable notion of input, for example, hours exposed to a language.

The next step was the development of the interaction hypothesis, which was presented first in Long's 1996 article on the role of the linguistic environment in second language acquisition. While this hypothesis was popular for some time in the 1990s, few informants mention it as a major trend.

### 7.1.2 Transfer and cross-linguistic influence

From its beginnings, applied linguists have looked at the impact of the first language on the language to be learned. Work by Terence Odlin and Eric Kellerman has continued the tradition of contrastive analysis, though in updated form. Kellerman's "psychotypology" concept has changed views on transfer as a purely mechanical copying of rules and elements from the first language into the second. Robert DeKeyser notices still some remnants of the old contrastive analysis tradition, but also less of an obsession with errors: "Language learning is more than avoiding errors."

A typical European development has been the study of learner varieties. Wolfgang Klein and Clive Perdue were most active in this research, which has led to a rethinking of what constitutes learner language. In a sense it is a move away from the interlanguage concept as developed by Selinker, because it is not focused on the development in the direction of a standard native speaker but has its own dynamic. The basic variety emerged from interaction between non-natives of a particular language, similar to pidgin and creole languages. In this context, Chris Candlin observes that the Klein and Perdue work never went well with British applied linguists, who look more at the social side than the psycholinguistic one.

Though not specific for research on input and interaction, Martin Bygate sees a tendency that

> people seem too ready to move on to something new, rather than stick with a particular problem and use empirical evidence in order to test and if necessary refine the formulation. For example, people working on the interaction hypothesis invariably produce results demonstrating that the input hypothesis is correct. Rare are those who bother to examine the limits of the hypothesis – whether in terms of the minimum levels of interaction needed for acquisition to take place, nor the maximum that

can be tolerated, nor how the hypothesis interacts with different kinds of learners (such as age, cultural background, educational background, or learning style) ... A similar point can be made about the concept "negotiation for meaning", which was central in the interaction hypothesis. The term "meaning" has multiple referents (morpheme meaning, phrasal meaning, clausal meaning, discoursal meaning, and overall pragmatic meaning, for example) so meaning can be negotiated at numerous levels, involving widely differing negotiation processes. So one trend is a sad one – the lack of careful formulation of theories, and a lack of commitment to investigating them critically and systematically.

### 7.1.3 *Language attrition and language loss*

Several informants (Theo van Els, Dick Lambert, Lydia White, Eric Kellerman) mention the growth of interest in non-pathological language decline as one of the main trends. The terminology on this is often confusing. The most widely accepted definitions see language attrition as the loss of language skills in individuals over time, language shift as the process of decline of use and incomplete transmission between generations, and language loss as the overarching term for the two.

Lambert and Freed's (1982) book on language attrition was the starting point for various researchers to work on language attrition. Originally, the research was political in nature with questions like "Why should we teach French for four years in high school and college when all that knowledge is lost so easily?" Later it became more cognitive in nature, with connections to psychological research on memory and forgetting through the work of people like Bert Weltens and Monika Schmid in the Netherlands, and Lynne Hansen at Brigham Young University.

Over the years, the research on language attrition has become more integrated with research on acquisition through the application of DST to language, which poses that language knowledge is never stable and that depending on the setting and frequency of use, phases of growth and decline may follow each other, and both are governed by the same principles.

A more recent trend is the interest in relearning languages. The assumption is that relearning a language is easier than learning a new language from scratch, but there is only limited research on this as yet.

### 7.1.4 *Individual differences*

The label "individual differences" typically refers to four aspects, namely:

- Age
- Attitudes and motivation
- Language aptitude
- Personality traits.

Of these, age and motivation are mentioned most often, and there seems to be hardly any interest in aptitude and personality traits. There is clearly more interest in individual differences, which has had an impact on research methodology: there is more interest in differences between learners and deviations from the mean are seen as relevant rather than noise. As Fred Genesee says: "There is a move from difference as deficit to difference as difference." This trend toward more individual pathways in learning has also led to a (renewed) interest in longitudinal studies. Maybe it is not really a trend, since longitudinal studies have been carried out regularly: from Merrill Swain's PhD study with the wonderful title 'Bilingualism as a first language' in 1972, to Cancino *et al.* (1978) to Spoelman and Verspoor (2010). The growing interest in complexity/dynamic systems theory has stimulated the use of dense data collection designs that allow for analysis at different timescales including the seconds and milliseconds that are analyzed in Conversational Analysis (CA). John Schumann has a bold proposal: "Maybe we should use the tools from CA for the analysis of dense longitudinal data without the philosophy of CA."

The age factor is certainly one of the topics that received extensive attention in the last decades. Though the idea that post-puberty learners can never reach a native level of proficiency is much older, the debate on what has become known as "the age factor" has been lively, to put it mildly. David Singleton observes: "People bow to the data. Hyltenstam no longer believes in the strong version of the critical period hypothesis and even Michael Long for a moment said 'I may be wrong' when confronted with data from Sonja van Boxtel's project."[1] The discussion seems to have shifted from some absolutist choice for or against the existence of a critical period for language learning, to whether an early start with learning foreign languages in primary education is beneficial and effective or not.

The interest in the role of motivation for language learning continued to be substantial, starting with the early work by Gardner, to Krashen's affective filter and to models of motivation in educational settings. Recently it has seen the most significant growth, mainly through the stimulating role of Zoltán Dörnyei. Dörnyei has recently connected his work on motivation to ideas from DST, changing motivation from a stable independent variable into a dynamic variable that interacts with other variables over time. Connected to this is a growing interest in the role of emotions or affect as a factor in language development and use.

Research on language aptitude has been less prevalent after the heyday when the Carroll and Sapon modern language aptitude test battery was popular. More recently, Paul Meara and his group developed a new aptitude test (LAT03) that has a solid theoretical basis and overlaps partly with the Pimsleur/Carroll/Sapon tests. The test is also available for young children. The debate about the role of intelligence separate from or as a component of other aptitude components continues. However, the interest in aptitude-treatment-interaction that was popular in the mid 1970s seems to have faded, though Robert DeKeyser mentions that he continues to work on this.

## 7.2 Sociolinguistic aspects: language in context

The term sociolinguistics is defined very broadly here; it is not just the study of varieties, but includes all aspects of language in context. Andrea Tyler refers to Ron Scollon for this, who sees no real distinction between AL and sociolinguistics. This view is clearly not shared by the majority of the informants, though there are certainly areas of overlap.

### 7.2.1 Multilingualism and L3

Multilingualism is en vogue, both in academia and in international organizations. At the European level, multilingualism is seen as one of the ways to promote a sense of European citizenship. But multilingualism comes in different guises.

According to Tove Skutnabb-Kangas:

> There has been a (positive) trend from seeing multilingualism as a deficit to seeing it as a resource, both in general and in education. This is part of a destructive either/or thinking (which has also taken the form of claiming that one has to choose between learning the mother tongue and the indigenous/minority culture, and become economically and politically marginalised), OR learn a dominant language at the cost of the mother tongue, subtractively – and get a good job.

Vivian Cook coined the concept of "multi-competence" that has become one of the buzzwords in the study of bilingualism and multilingualism. The main idea is that the bilingual (or trilingual, quadrilingual and so on) is not two monolinguals in one, or two separate languages in one brain. The acquisition of a second language leads to a reorganization of the language system with the different languages influencing each other. For Aneta Pavlenko, "Vivian Cook is a visionary who made major efforts to bring together multilingualism, and European and North American SLA efforts, as well as UG and cognitive linguistics". In contrast to the traditional perspectives of interference or transfer as a one-directional process from L1 to L2, the L1 is as amenable to influences from other languages, in similar ways as the L2 is. Camilla Bardel thinks the multi-competence trend has brought the notion of transfer back into the discussion but now not only from L1 into L2 but in multiple ways between L1/L2/L3/ … with all languages affecting the others. This perspective on multilingualism also implies that the role of the native speaker changes, as mentioned earlier by Alan Davies. In research on multilingual processing, using monolingual native speakers as a control or reference group is no longer seen as acceptable. It is better to compare multilinguals at different stages of their development.

In research on L3 there has been an elaborate discussion on what counts as the first/second/third language. Is it the order of acquisition, the level of proficiency, the frequency of current use or the individual's preference that should be the criterion? As Suzanne Flynn remarks, the study of trilinguals allows us to study phenomena that we cannot study in bilinguals. María del Pilar García Mayo says: "I think L3 research will probably emerge as a very important trend in the years to come."

The L3 community has grown considerably in the last decade with its own journal (*International Journal of Multilingualism*), and books and conferences dedicated to this theme. Whether or not trilingualism is fundamentally different from bilingualism in terms of psycholinguistic processes is a matter of debate.

Several informants (Suresh Canagarajah, Sinfree Makoni, Alastair Pennycook) have proposed radically different perspectives on language and languages in a multilingual world. In their view, our conception of language needs to be reconceptualized. Suresh Canagarajah points to the effect of massive migration and mobility: "Language is a mobile resource that tended to be linked to territories, but need no longer be." For Elizabeth Lanza:

> the influence of approaches that bring in globalization and mobility and problematize various views of language have abounded, cf. translanguaging, the unboundedness of language. Notions of the fluidity of language and the deconstruction of language as a system flourish in current sociolinguistic thinking.

### 7.2.2 Language shift

Language shift typically takes place in migration settings. Due to the interaction with the dominant language, the original mother tongue is used less and is structurally influenced by that language. Patterns of use often change with the second generation migrants shifting to the dominant language outside the home. Education also plays a role since the original mother tongue is seldom taught or even allowed in educational settings. In the United States, many heritage language users who have been brought up partially in the other language are trying to maintain that language, and language maintenance and revival, are becoming core issues in language policy, as Terrence Wiley mentions. Still, Rosamond Mitchell sees a "weak response to language loss/language death around the world". Tove Skutnabb-Kangas strongly agrees.

### 7.2.3 Language and identity

The growing interest in identity as a factor is one of the main trends in AL, but not everybody is particularly pleased with that development. Merrill Swain complains: "Now everything is about identity." Talking about the booming interest in identity, Terrence Wiley jokingly suggested that we need a *Journal of Narcissism*. He recalls one study submitted to a journal on the construction of identity in one essay in a third grade ESL class. Though generalization may not be the chief aim of such studies, he wonders what their relevance is.

Aneta Pavlenko has changed her perspective on the post-structuralist views on identity:

> Post-structuralism had a mixed effect on the field. On the positive side, it opened new directions for scholarly inquiry and enriched our under- standing of the social, political and economic aspects of second language learning and use. On the negative side, it gave rise to a lot of fluff, that is, meaningless "studies" that continued to make the same point over and over (identities are multiple and dynamic) and contributed little if any- thing to our knowledge base. If there is anything I regret about my career, it is contributing to this trend – if I could "unpublish" some of my own identity work, I would happily do so.

### 7.2.4 The spread of English and English as a Lingua Franca (ELF)

A pervasive trend has been the spread of English all over the world. Jodi Crandall points to the many "unintended consequences". Different schools of thought and action on this topic have emerged, such as the English as a Lingua Franca (ELF) group and the World Englishes group. One of the informants who writes extensively about this issue is Tove Skutnabb-Kangas:

> Of course I am worried about the completely uncritical subtractive spreading of English. People could learn English additively and it has been shown with massive, both smaller and large-scale studies that mother-tongue-based multilingual education leads to good results (which subtractive submersion doesn't do) – still the work of apologists of subtractive English (or other "big" languages) continues. Politicians don't read research. AL hasn't been helpful in this.

One of the growing areas of research in the last decade is on the develop- ment of English as an international language to ELF. One of the main leaders is Barbara Seidlhofer, who has set up various projects together with her colleagues in Vienna, including a corpus of ELF interactions. One pedagogic implication of ELF research is the questioning of the native speaker as the sole goal or reference in English language teaching. The essence of the ELF movement is the removing of the native speaker as the goal or reference in language learning. The focus on the native speaker is still prevalent, despite many publications denouncing it. The focus on the native speaker is also visible in the wordings of the Common European Framework of Reference (CEFR) "can-do" statements, which makes this framework less relevant for ELF. ELF speakers are essentially using the language to get things done and are typically non-native speakers. As Barbara Seidlhofer mentions, "having a C2 level may be a hindrance rather than an asset in communication with speakers with lower levels of proficiency". Related to this, Ben Rampton sees "the erosion of an exclusive Anglo perspective, and the challenge to native-speaker ascendancy". Paul Meara sees this "as the move away from Britain and the USA as the fountains of all knowledge". According to Tim McNamara ELF is the biggest challenge facing the testing world, which, in his view, tends to be quite conservative. The ELF movement undermines some of the key assumptions current language testing is based on. But not all informants agree with this. Robert Philipson: "I am worried that a considerable amount of fashionable research of the kind that Blommaert, Pennycook, and the ELF gospel and others are churning out is intellectual games rather than concerned with existential issues for language learners or language policies."

### 7.2.5 Variation and variability

A distinction is often made between intra-individual variability and inter-individual variation. The interest in variability and variation in interlanguage has grown, according to Robert DeKeyser, as has the awareness of the dependence of variation on task and individual. There is a rich literature and a well-tested methodology in sociolinguistics for the analysis of variation (VARBRUL) and Elaine Tarone deplores that applied linguists have not taken advantage of that in the study of SLA. In her view, variation in development can be studied with VARBRUL, though the software does not allow for the analysis of the interaction of variables over time, which would be the focus in a CDST-based analysis of variation.

In the early days of SLA, studies on morpheme orders were very popular and the conclusion of those studies was that the first language does not really play a role in SLA, as all learners go through the same order or stages, independent of their first language. John Schumann argues that such universal orders are arrived at by eliminating variation:

> Let's suppose that the sequence for the acquisition of English negation is universally true. How did we arrive at that? We accomplished that by abstracting from the individual variation. The initial research involves six different case studies – two children, two adolescents, and two adults. We determine the acquisition for each individual by, for each sample, taking the total number of negative utterances and dividing that figure into the number of each negative form – excluding "*I don't know*" and negative phrases (we only considered verbal negation). The form with the highest percentage was seen as characteristic of the sample as a whole. In every sample each subject had a variety of negative forms, hence variation was recognized, but largely ignored. On the basis of this analysis, we then constructed a common sequence.

Similar remarks have been made about various studies that claim fixed acquisition orders. Variation takes another perspective when looked at not as noise but as information, as CT/DST analyses show.

### 7.2.6 Language policy

According to Joseph Lo Bianco: "Language planning theory and language planning was repudiated in the mid to late 1990s, has made a major comeback in recent years, much stronger in theory but still needs more work." Elizabeth Lanza mentions that "in language policy research, a move has been from examining macro language policy as seen in institutional structures and documents to considering language policy as linguistic practices. A shift from macro to micro." As Terrence Wiley indicates, the AL research agenda, in particular with respect to English as a second language, but increasingly so for foreign languages, has been dictated by national and federal goals. As he mentions, most interest in language policy issues in the United States now comes from the Department of Defence and Homeland Security, while financial support from the Department of Education is almost non-existent. This had partly to do with post-9/11 developments and partly with the move against multiculturalism, which made labels like bilingual education and immersion almost taboo words. According to Michael Long:

> In the USA, many individuals in the field have a positive impact locally, e.g., through personal friendships opening doors with influential policy makers at the school board level. In my opinion, the situation at the national level is different, however, with so-called "proficiency scales" and the under-examined notion of proficiency itself, having a stultifying effect on national language policy and government language programs.

Dick Tucker points to AL involvement with language planning for indigenous and heritage language learning. He also mentions "the need for attention for articulation between levels and CLIL". Articulation between levels refers to how the competences acquired in primary school fit in with the competences required in secondary education. In the Netherlands this is a core issue, related to the CLIL/bilingual education development: when CLIL in primary education catches on, more and more children will enter secondary education with fairly advanced levels of proficiency in English, which means that English teachers in secondary are faced with on the one hand pupils with hardly any proficiency in English and on the other hand pupils with a good command of at least spoken English. This calls for differentiation in the classroom, something that not all teachers are equally prepared for.

In the European context, the European Union treaty of Barcelona clearly has had an impact on the AL research agenda. The main goals of the European language policy are to make larger sections of its citizens trilingual, with two foreign languages in addition to the mother tongue. The approaches needed to reach that goal are an early start with foreign language teaching, preferably from age four in primary education, and a teaching approach in which the learning of content and language is integrated (CLIL). Interestingly, these developments have led to a range of projects on the benefits of an early start with foreign languages and the effectiveness of the CLIL approach, which linked up with developments on content based instruction and sheltered language programs in the United States and Canada.

A special example of the link between national policies and AL is the case of testing in Israel. Elana Shohamy remembers she just could not sleep due to the responsibility she felt for a test of spoken Hebrew, which, after its introduction appeared to have a massive washback effect on language teaching, in the sense that all of a sudden the instruction of language production became a priority, affecting everything from teacher education to material design. She also mentions with sadness that the tests were often applied to people who were to be expelled anyway. Howard Nicholas mentions the huge contribution to language policy of the late Michael Clyne: "As much as applied linguistics is a multifaceted term and its relationship to linguistics contested, Michael Clyne was a central bridging and intellectual figure." He also was the driving force behind the inclusion of language questions in the Australian national census, which led to similar actions in various other countries.

Though probably not typical of the field of language policy, Terrence Wiley sees a lot of what he calls "salt and pepper references", references that fit all sizes and topics. Foucault is a favorite in this respect. As mentioned in Chapter 5, several other informants mention the tendency toward black boxing, giving stretches of references to support a point while in fact many of the references either are conceptually and methodologically weak or hardly related to the point they are supposed to support.

In this analysis the role of institutions and organizations is not treated in any detail, there are other studies (Catford, Grabe, Kaplan) that did so. Some people, however, did comment on this. Rosamond Mitchell says: "There is a great increase in scale of activity, but continuing domination of the field by research led institutions in a smallish number of countries."

Based on lifelong experience, Fred Genesee comments on the relation with educational authorities:

> In education they take language research serious, and educators feel at least compelled to listen to me because they believe that science has something useful to say about how first and second languages are learned. This, in turn, they believe should inform their educational policies and practices.

But dealing with policy makers is different:

> We often don't know how to talk with policy makers; we talk to them as if the only considerations when making decisions are logical – what

research says and, thus, what they should do. However, they are often influenced by political or community concerns that override the more rational view that we as researchers take. For this reason, I think we have not always been very effective in our discussions with them.

According to Bill VanPatten, the impact of AL on language education is limited: "Language education is not controlled by AL in the US."
Jan Hulstijn sees the development of credit systems as an important trend:

A massive impact has had, however, the Council of Europe's enterprise to arrive at a European Unit Credit System for Modern Language Learning by Adults, starting with the Rüschlikon Congress in 1971, reaching a first peak with the publication of the Threshold Level (Van Ek, 1975), and culminating in the publication of the Common European Framework of Reference (CEFR) in its final version in 2001.

The notion that, in his view, this is an important trend does not imply that he fully endorses the ideas behind the CEFR and its current applications. He talks about "the shaky ground beneath the CEFR" in an early paper on this topic. As mentioned earlier, not all informants see the development and spread of the CEFR as a positive development. Although he sees the CEFR as a good development, David Singleton worries about its basis in research.

### 7.2.7 The linguistic landscape

In the last decade many researchers have been attracted by the research on language in spaces, in particular the linguistic landscape. The research on this was stimulated by Ben-Rafael and Shohamy in the Israeli/West Bank context. They showed how public signs, but also advertisements and shop windows reflect the distribution of power through the languages that are visible. Joan Kelly Hall thinks that "the idea of linguistic landscape is captivating; it can be used in classrooms to ask real questions about how language is used". There have been several special symposia on this topic at AAAL (the American Association of Applied Linguistics) and AILA (Association Internationale Linguistique Appliquée) conferences, and a number of books and special issues of journals have been devoted to it, with work by Jasone Cenoz, Nick Coupland, Durk Gorter, Bernard Spolsky, Aneta Pavlenko and Christopher Stroud.

## 7.3 Educational aspects

A non-trivial aspect mentioned regularly is that there is no one-size-fits-all method of teaching. Or, as Alister Cumming put it: "Recognition of the complex, variable, and multi-faceted dimensions of language learning and of education rather than any preferred, singular teaching method or uniform progression of SLA." The relation between AL and language teaching continues to be complex. Celeste Kinginger feels that she "has to believe that there is a role for AL in language teaching, if only as a catalyst for change when the surrounding circumstances permit".

### 7.3.1 Vocabulary acquisition

A small but very active group of researchers has done extensive research on vocabulary. The research on vocabulary has exploded as Paul Meara found out when he wanted to continue his very useful bibliographies on vocabulary (www.lognostics.co.uk/varga): they have grown exponentially and it is basically impossible now to try to be complete. Research on vocabulary serves as an intersection between areas such as reading and literacy and AL, and as such is a strong connection point between fields.

Paul Nation notes that:

> there has been an enormous revival in attention to vocabulary. Over 30 per cent of the vocabulary research in the last 100 years has appeared in the last ten years. In spite of this, AL theory has little to say about vocabulary and grammar dominates.

Norbert Schmitt mentions that traditional linguistics theory did not focus on vocabulary, and adds that there is still no overall theory of vocabulary acquisition. But the newer usage based theories do provide useful guidance on the role of frequency of input on vocabulary acquisition. However, he points out that research has shown, at least in L2 contexts, that the frequency of input (and often the saliency as well) is not enough to ensure acquisition of the large amounts of vocabulary necessary to use a language well. Thus, vocabulary needs to be taught in a principled way, with some explicit instruction, while maximizing exposure both in and outside the classroom (e.g. by extensive reading). Part of this approach includes the move from single word learning to learning formulaic sequences or what Smiskova-Gustafsson (2013) calls Conventional Ways of Saying Things (CWOSTS). Also, the use of corpus analysis can be a useful guide in the principled selection of words to be learned, rather than relying solely on a teacher's intuition.

### 7.3.2 Task-based language teaching (TBLT)

While task-based learning is seen as a major development in language teaching, the research it is supposedly based on is not seen as very strong generally. Albert Weideman comments that task complexity cannot be defined and that the way a task is used in teaching is much more relevant. Martin Bygate comments:

People working within TBLT rarely come up with limitations on the use of tasks in the classroom, or on the use of different types of task. To some extent those working within the cognition hypothesis have found negative results, but some seem rarely to seek out negative results, and where they have occurred, have often seemed to prefer to explain them away.

According to Johannes Wagner "TBLT has been very influential, partly because it picked up some formats which L2 learners already used before they could give it a name."

### 7.3.3 Teacher education

According to Karen Johnson, teacher trainers are typically seen as responsible for the transfer of findings from AL research into classrooms. Many informants notice that so many useful ideas and findings are left untouched by language teachers, and they blame it on the teacher trainers who seem to be more concerned about adolescent psychology and classroom management than with innovating language teaching. According to Jim Lantolf, many teachers lack a fundamental and deep understanding of the language they are teaching. The focus is primarily on fluency. There is generally little concern for the beginning teacher who has to survive in her classroom and who is typically domesticated by the older teachers in the team, and who then has to improve language teaching according to applied linguists' findings. Donald Freeman sees a "shift from thinking of teaching as a matter of behavior, and therefore solely as 'trainable', to thinking of teaching as social activity, and therefore involving individual and collective sense making". This is endorsed by Bernd Rüsschoff, who says: "One might mention the fact that in FLA the major trend has been a shift from an instructivist, teacher-controlled classroom towards more cooperative and collaborative learning arrangements, in which teacher and learners act as partners-in-learning." Gabriele Kasper argues that research in AL and other disciplines has led to the availability of instruments that may improve language teaching. She sees the potential of an approach in teacher education in which teachers are given the tools to evaluate their own behavior. CA tools could help teachers in understanding the interactions with their students better. Teachers should not be told what to do, but made aware of what they do. Such "teacher empowerment" could be seen as the result of AL research according to Diane Larsen-Freeman:

> There has been a tendency in AL to say to teachers: "We figure things out and you use them". It is much more effective to do research together with teachers than to dictate to them, or at least to include teachers' questions on our research agenda.

## 7.4 Conclusion

This chapter presented psycholinguistic, sociolinguistic and educational trends as mentioned by the informants. They have been organized along the lines of psycholinguistic, sociolinguistic and educational. It is difficult to draw conclusions on such a wide range of topics. Some of the topics are interrelated, others stand alone. The tendency seems to be to compartmentalize and further specialize, with less content left in the center. On the educational side there is communicative language learning and task-based teaching, both receiving lukewarm reactions from the informants. CLIL is seen as an important development, at least in the European context.

In the decades covered in this study, the link between psycholinguistics and sociolinguistics has been weak, with each focusing on its own issues. The link between educational aspects and psycholinguistics was virtually non-existent, despite the often obligatory references to improvement of language teaching in psycholinguistic studies. There are many sociolinguistic studies on language classrooms and other educational settings, but even there the relevance of the findings for practitioners is often limited.

## Note

1 The occasion was the farewell workshop for Theo Bongaerts in June 2008.

## References

Cancino, H., Rosansky, E. and Schumann, J. (1978) "The acquisition of English negatives and interrogatives by native Spanish speakers" in: E. Hatch (ed.), *Second Language Acquisition*, Rowley, MA: Newbury House, pp. 207–30.

Catford, J. (1998) "Language learning and applied linguistics: a historical sketch", *Language Learning*, vol. 48, no. 4: 465–96.

Grabe, W. (2002) "Applied linguistics: An emerging discipline for the twenty-first century" in: R. Kaplan (ed.) *The Oxford Handbook of Applied Linguistics*, Oxford: Oxford University Press, pp. 3–12.

Kaplan, R. (ed.) (2010) *The Oxford Handbook of Applied Linguistics*, 2nd edn, Oxford: Oxford University Press.

Lambert, R. and Freed, B. (1982) *The Loss of Language Skills*, Rowley, MA: Newbury House.

Long, M. (1996) "The role of the linguistic environment in second language acquisition" in: W. Ritchie and T. Bhatia (eds), *Handbook of Second Language Acquisition*, San Diego: Academic Press, pp. 413–68.

Smiskova-Gustafsson, H. (2013) "Formulaic sequences in second language acquisition", *LOT* PhD thesis, Groningen: University of Groningen.

Spoelman, M. and Verspoor, M. (2010) "Dynamic patterns in the development of accuracy and complexity: A longitudinal case study on the acquisition of Finnish", *Applied Linguistics*, vol. 31, no. 4: 532–53.

Swain, M. (1972) "Bilingualism as a first language", PhD dissertation, UCLA.

van Ek, J. (1975) "The threshold level", *Education and Culture*, vol. 28: 21–6.

# 8 Trends III

## The dynamic turn

As mentioned in the previous chapters, one of the great changes or trends in the last decades has been what is called "the social turn", which reflects the awareness that language development is not a solitary cognitive activity but one that is embedded, connected and embodied. Though this social turn represented a significant shift in perspective, it was not what in Kuhnian terms would be called a paradigm shift. Even though some of the points of difference were difficult to incorporate into the status quo at the time, the field was flexible enough to adopt and integrate this new development. However, Complex Dynamic Systems Theory (CDST) is different. Many of the informants see CDST as the new paradigm that fills the gap left by formal linguistic models, the disembodied psycholinguistic approach and various theories that either look exclusively at the psycholinguistic side or at the sociolinguistic and sociocultural side only.

This chapter is different from the other chapters on trends in that it is more of my own voice than that of my informants that will be represented here. In this chapter it will be argued that the end of the period covered in this overview has seen the beginning of what is likely a real paradigm shift: *the dynamic turn*. I will argue that CDST does represent a paradigm shift and is relevant to many aspects of AL. I will also argue that the CDST perspective provides us with concepts and tools for various aspects of AL that other theories have not been able to deal with. The topics reflect my own interests and areas of expertise, and it is entirely possible that other areas could also benefit from a CDST approach. As Diane Larsen-Freeman (p.c.) suggests, CDST has been taken up in language planning and policy, instructional technology, English as a lingua franca, language awareness and teacher cognition, to name only some of the newer applications.

In this chapter I will try to show that CDST is relevant for many aspects of AL, with a focus on bilingual processing and code switching, variation in SLD and the role of motivation. First I will briefly sketch the development of CDST and its main components.

## 8.1 Complex Dynamic Systems Theory (CDST)

Though the emergence of CDST has a long history in mathematics and the hard sciences, the interest from an AL perspective started with Diane

Larsen-Freeman's seminal article in *Applied Linguistics* in 1997. As she mentions, it took a while for this line of thinking to be seen as an important development. Seeing language as a complex adaptive system and second language development as a dynamic process has profoundly shifted our understanding of both. A target language is no longer seen as a static target representation, to which learners increasingly conform. In its place, language and its use are mutually constitutive; they determine each other. It is in situated, co-adaptive, discursive encounters that learners obtain relevant and accessible exemplars from which they can learn. Language use, change and learning take place on multiple timescales and levels of complexity. They are temporally and contextually dependent processes.

This view has substantial implications for methodology. One is a new appreciation for variation in the data, which is seen as providing information rather than clouding the "real data". Because individuals differ in their developmental paths, longitudinal case studies are encouraged; they provide a different picture of development than group studies and cross-sectional studies, which tend to disregard variation by focusing more on central tendencies. Rather than isolating a single variable, researchers look for patterns among interacting factors, whereby some factors have more influence at certain times than others. The interconnectedness of embedded subsystems in a language means that changes in one system may lead to changes in other systems.

Because of different initial conditions and the uniqueness of each learner, the same, shared input may lead to different, individual outcomes. Because of this non-linearity, development trajectories may not be predictable, although they should be explicable retrospectively. Simple causal statements give way to contingent statements, and rules give way to patterns. CDST is not a theory of language. Theories of language that are theoretically consistent with it are Cognitive Linguistics and Systemic Functional Linguistics. Both underscore the dynamic nature of language and understand language as a socio-cognitive construct, deriving from embodied experience. Also aligned with CDST is an emergentist or usage based approach to language development. Karlfried Knapp sees as one of the significant trends the move from seeing language as "a more or less stable formal system to viewing it as a dynamic, adaptive process-oriented system whose acquisition is usage-based". This view is endorsed by many informants, including Zoltán Dörnyei, Jean-Marc Dewaele, Aneta Pavlenko and John Schumann. Diane Larsen-Freeman also expresses her worries about this new perspective: "It is difficult to convey the power of this new approach to conceiving familiar phenomena. Ironically, we are limited by our language itself in reflecting its dynamicity." Rod Ellis is yet to be convinced of the relevance and impact of CDST. In his view, the interconnectedness between components should include a link between the social, the cognitive and the linguistic aspects of language use. So far, no study has shown that convincingly. The question is what the definition of a theory is. Is CDST a theory, as some of its proponents claim, or a useful metaphor? Rod Ellis's ideas are shared by Henry Widdowson, who asks: "What complexity is there that we cannot explain using socio-linguistic notions of variation and mental schemata as proposed by Uriel Neisser in the 1960s?" For him, the development of dynamism and complexity does not come as a surprise, since in the social sciences we have always known that everything changes constantly through the impact of social and individual factors. "Projections of individuals in interaction has been common knowledge for quite some time, adapting to all the changing factors in interaction", says Henry Widdowson. Rod Ellis indicates that he is not convinced that this theory will actually help to understand the basic issues in language learning and teaching, although Diane Larsen-Freeman has already pointed to iterative adaptation as a way of characterizing language learning and practices such as iteration, rather than repetition, and teaching adaptation, as having consequences for pedagogy.

In the last decade a number of books and special issues of journals have played a role in the development of this approach, including de Bot *et al.* (2005, 2007), Larsen-Freeman and Cameron (2008), Dörnyei (2009) and Verspoor *et al.* (2011). Through these publications and reactions to them a list of the main characteristics of complex dynamic systems as relevant for SLD have emerged. The list contains the following characteristics:

- CDST is the science of the development of complex systems over time. Complex systems are sets of interacting variables from which emerges something novel.
- In many complex systems the outcome of development over time cannot be predicted, not because we lack the right tools to measure it, but because the variables that interact and their influence keep changing over time.
- Dynamic systems are always part of another system, with systems nested within other systems, ranging in levels from sub-molecular particles to the universe.
- Systems develop through iterations of simple procedures that are applied over and over again with the output of one preceding iteration serving as the input of the next.
- Complexity emerges out of the iterative application of simple procedures; therefore, it is not necessary to postulate innate knowledge.
- The development of a dynamic system appears to be highly dependent on its initial state. Minor differences at the beginning can have dramatic consequences in the long run.
- In dynamic systems, changes in one variable have an impact on all other variables that are part of the system: systems are fully interconnected.
- Development is dependent on resources. All natural systems will tend to entropy when no additional energy matter or information is added to the system.

- Systems develop through interaction with their environment and through internal self-reorganization.
- Because systems are constantly in flux, they will show variation, they are sensitive to specific input at a given point in time and other input at another point in time.
- The cognitive system as a dynamic system is typically *situated*, i.e. closely connected to a specific here and now situation, *embodied*, i.e. cognition is not just the computations that take place in the brain but also includes interactions with the rest of the human body, and *distributed*: "Knowledge is socially constructed through collaborative efforts to achieve shared objectives in cultural surroundings" (Salomon 1993: 1).

Van Gelder (1998) describes how a CDST perspective on cognition differs from a more traditional one:

> The cognitive system is not a discrete sequential manipulator of static representational structures: rather, it is a structure of mutually and simultaneously influencing change. Its processes do not take place in the arbitrary, discrete time of computer steps: rather, they unfold in the real time of ongoing change in the environment, the body, and the nervous system. The cognitive system does not interact with other aspects of the world by passing messages and commands: rather, it continuously coevolves with them.
>
> (3)

As mentioned before, CDST regards variation in the data as a source of useful information rather than noise that clouds the "real data". The interconnectedness of embedded systems means that changes in one system may lead to changes in other systems. Development may not be predictable, and the same input may lead to different outcomes depending on initial conditions. Because individuals differ so much in their developmental paths, group studies and cross-sectional designs are seen as less relevant than longitudinal case studies.

Below, some topics to which a CDST perspective can be applied will be dealt with in more detail, although CDST is applicable to many topics. The topics dealt with are the psycholinguistic approach to bilingualism and multilingualism and the inadequacy of some of its basic assumptions, code-switching as a dynamic process and dynamic perspectives on individual differences in language development.

## 8.2  CDST and multilingual processing[1]

The rise of the view of language as a CDS has cast doubt on the validity of the more traditional models discussed so far (see Lowie and Verspoor (2011) for a discussion). The main problem is that these models are based on underlying assumptions that may no longer be tenable:

- Language processing is modular: it is carried out by a number of cognitive modules that have their own specific input and output and that function more or less autonomously.
- Language processing is incremental and there is no internal feedback or feedforward.
- Isolated elements (phonemes, words, sentences) are studied without taking into account the larger linguistics and social context they are part of.
- For language production: based on individual monologue rather than interaction as the default speaking situation.
- Language processing involves operations on invariant and abstract representations.

Because of these underlying assumptions, isolated elements (phonemes, words, sentences) are studied without taking into account the larger linguistic and social context they are part of. Also, the models are static and steady state models in which change over time has no role to play. Moreover, studies are based on individual monologue rather than interaction as the default speaking situation.

Within the tradition such models are part of, these characteristics may be unproblematic, but in recent years new perspectives on cognition have developed that lead to a different view. The most important development is the emergence of the dynamic perspective on cognition in general and language processing in particular. The most important tenet is that any open complex system (such as the bilingual mind) interacts continuously with its environment and will continuously change over time. With these notions in mind, let us look at each characteristic of traditional models as outlined above in more detail:

- Language processing is modular: it is carried out by a number of cognitive modules that have their own specific input and output and that function more or less autonomously.

The most outspoken opponent of a modular approach to cognitive processing at the moment is probably Michael Spivey in his book *The Continuity of Mind* (2007). His main argument is that there is substantial evidence against the existence of separate modules for specific cognitive activities, such as face recognition and object recognition. For linguistic theories this is crucial, since in UG based theories a separate and innate language module plays a central role. Distributed processing of language undermines the idea that language is uniquely human and innate because the cooperating parts of the brain are not unique for language and have no specific linguistic knowledge.

- Language processing is incremental and there is no internal feedback or feedforward.

One of the problems of this assumption is that many second language speakers regularly experience a "feeling of knowing". They want to say something in the foreign language, but are aware of the fact that they do not know or have quick access to a word they are going to need to finish a sentence (de Bot 2004). This suggests at least some form of feedforward in speaking. Additional evidence against a strict incremental view is provided in an interesting experiment by Hald *et al.* (2006). In this experiment, speaker characteristics (social dialect) and speech characteristics (high/low cultural content) were distributed in such a way that speaker and speech characteristics were orthogonally varied. Listeners heard speakers whose dialect clearly showed their high or low socio-economic status talk about Chopin's piano music or about tattoos. The combinations of high cultural content and low social status in a neuro-imaging experiment led to N400 reactions, which showed that these utterances were experienced as deviant. A comparison with similar sentences with grammatical deviations showed that the semantic errors were detected earlier than the syntactic ones, which is a problem for a purely incremental process from semantics to syntax and phonology. The semantics and pragmatics seem to override the syntax in this experiment.

- Isolated elements (phonemes, words, sentences) are studied without taking into account the larger linguistics and social context they are part of.

If cognition is situated, embodied and distributed, studying isolated elements is fairly pointless: we need to investigate them as they relate to other aspects of the larger context, both linguistic and extra-linguistic. For example, work by Eisner and McQueen (2006) has shown that the perception of ambiguous phonemes is strongly influenced by the semantics of the context in which that phoneme is used.

- For language production: based on individual monologue rather than interaction as the default speaking situation.

As Pickering and Garrod (2004) have argued, we should move away from monologue as the default type of language production and look at interaction instead. The task for a speaker is fundamentally different in interaction as compared to monologue. The literature on syntactic priming supports this way of looking at production: how language is used depends only partly on the intentions and activities of individual speakers and is to a large extent defined by the characteristics of the interaction.

- Language processing involves operations on invariant and abstract representations.

In the models presented earlier, and in the information processing approach in general the assumption is that language processing is the manipulation of invariant entities (words, phonemes, syntactic patterns). In a dynamic approach this invariance is highly problematic because every use of a word, expression or construction will have an impact on the way it is represented in the brain. As Spivey (2007) indicates: "I contend that cognitive psychology's traditional information processing approach ... places too much emphasis on easily labeled static representations that are claimed to be computed at intermittently stable periods over time" (4). He admits that static representations are the cornerstone of the information processing approach and that it will be difficult to replace them with a concept that is more dynamic because what we have now is too vague and underspecified.

So far there is hardly any research on the stability of linguistic representations. De Bot and Lowie (2010) report on an experiment in which a simple word-naming task of high frequency words was used. The outcomes show that correlations between different sessions with the same subject and between subjects were very low. In other words, a word that was reacted to fast in one session could have a slow reaction in another session or individual. This points to variation that is inherent in the lexicon and that results from contact interaction and reorganization of elements in networks. Elman (2005) phrases this as follows:

> We might choose to think of the internal state that the network is in when it processes a word as representing that word (in context), but it is more accurate to think of that state as the *result* of processing the word rather than as a representation of the word itself.
>
> (207)

Additional evidence for the changeability of words and their meanings comes from an ERP study by Nieuwland and Van Berkum (2006) who compared ERP data for sentences like "The peanut was in love" versus "The peanut was salted". This type of anomaly typically leads to N400 reactions. Then they presented the subjects with a story about a peanut that falls in love. After listening to these stories, the N400 effects disappeared, which shows that through discourse information the basic semantic aspects of words can be changed.

## 8.3 Characteristics of CDST-based models of bilingual processing

As may be clear from the argumentation so far, we may have to review some of the basic assumptions of the information processing approach on which our current models of multilingual processing are based. In the previous section we have listed the main characteristics of these models and outlined the problems related to them. From this follows that we need to develop models that take into account the dynamic perspective in which time and change are the core issues. As Spivey (2007) argues:

The fundamental weakness of some of the major experimental techniques in cognitive psychology and neuroscience is that they ignore much of the time course of processing and the gradual accumulation of partial information, focusing instead on the outcome of a cognitive process rather than the dynamic properties of that process.

(53)

The dynamic turn will lead to a rethinking of what is relevant in the study of multilingual processing. The psycholinguistic research as it has evolved over the last decade has become completely isolated from normal everyday language use; it looks at isolated words or phrases, with a focus on ecologically invalid tasks with yes/no responses, without taking into account the embodied and distributed nature of language use.

## 8.4 Code switching (CS) as language production

The second topic that will be considered from a CDST perspective is code switching (CS). CS mostly refers to switching between languages, but it also applies to dialects, and probably also styles and registers. When talking to neighbors a different style is used than when talking to an official person, like the mayor of the town. Essentially, switching registers is no different from switching languages. In that sense, there are probably no real monolinguals, since no one is completely monostylistic.

### 8.4.1 Sources of triggering in code switching[2]

Decades of research have taught us a lot about why people code switch in certain situations, but it is still largely unclear why particular instances of code switching occur where they do. There is abundant evidence for general effects of language proficiency, interactional setting, group affiliation, typological distance between languages and various other factors that affect global patterns of CS. But how these general factors are related to actual switches is unclear, and according to Sankoff (1998) it is not possible to predict each and every switch:

> Even if we can determine where a code-switch can occur and where it cannot, there is no way of knowing in advance for any site whether a switch will occur there or not. In particular, if a switch occurs at some point in a sentence, this does not constrain any potential site(s) later in the sentence either to contain another switch or not to – there are *no forced switches*.

(39, italics in original)

Still, we would want to know what the limits of this unpredictability are. There may be real time factors that have a direct impact on the language used in speech in a setting in which CS is a normal and generally accepted phenomenon. In CS "triggering" appears to play a role. First, we want to argue that CS is a very special type of bilingual language use and that it shows characteristics of what in physics has been described as a "critical state".

### 8.4.2 CS as a critical state

In bilingual language production, speakers will in most cases stick to the language that is most appropriate in a given setting. In some settings the use of more than one language may be called for. In that sense, CS is a normal way of speaking for many bilinguals but not the default in bilingual language production. It is a unique setting in which both languages − if we restrict ourselves to bilingual as opposed to multilingual situations − are activated to a very high level. Both languages are in Green's (1993: 263) terms "selected", that is, controlling speech output. In a CS setting switching between languages is the conversational norm, which means that there is a constant need to switch. The amount and type of switching is highly dependent on the conversational setting. In some settings minimal CS, such as pronouncing a word using the sounds of the other language, is enough to signal group adherence, in other settings longer stretches of speech are switched. This means that the social setting will push the language system in a critical state, that is, close to phase transition. In physics a whole field of research on phase transition has emerged and there is growing interest in what has been labeled "self-organized criticality" (SOC), a concept that has been coined by Bak *et al.* (1987) and developed further in Bak's (1996) book *How Nature Works: The Science of Self-organized Criticality*. The central idea which is based on CDST principles, is that systems develop through interaction with their environment and through internal reorganization and tend to be attracted to critical states in which a minor change can have unpredictable effects on the system. The metaphor Bak used was that of a sand pile: sand is dripping onto a smooth surface and forms a pile. As grains of sand are added one after the other, the slope of the pile will get steeper and steeper. Then at some point, adding one more grain of sand will cause an avalanche. When an avalanche will take place, how big it will be and where it will go cannot be predicted. After each avalanche, the system will be in a temporary state of balance until the next avalanche occurs. SOC is a property of (classes of) dynamical systems, which have a critical point as an attractor state. To quote Bak:

> I will argue that complex behavior in nature reflects the tendency of large systems with many components to evolve into a poised, "critical" state, way out of balance, where minor disturbances may lead to events, called avalanches, of all sizes. Most of the changes take place through catastrophic events rather than by following a smooth gradual path. The evolution to this very delicate state occurs without design from any

outside agent; the state is established solely because of the dynamical interactions among individual elements of the system: the critical state is *self-organized*. Self-organized criticality is so far the only known general mechanism to generate complexity.

(1996: 1–2)

Bak's ideas have been applied to many different fields, ranging from economics to epidemics, and visual attention to landscape formation. While the mathematics of SOC are well beyond the scope of the present contribution, some of the thinking on SOC seems to be applicable to the study of language development and language use, and in particular to CS. It can be argued that in a CS setting, the individual's language system tends to be attracted to a critical state in which the transition from one state (speaking language A, $L_a$) to another state (speaking language B, $L_b$) appears to be highly unpredictable, but not random. Many different sociolinguistic and psycholinguistic factors interact in the selection of the language of a specific utterance or part of that. But even if we accept that this line of thinking supports Sankoff's assumption on the unpredictability of CS, we still want to find out what might have led to a specific set of switches. Even if we cannot predict specific CSs, we may learn more about the phenomenon by looking at it "retrodictively", to use Larsen-Freeman's (2009) term. That is, we may be able to look back at what happened and point out what factors may have played a role in a specific instance, but we cannot claim that the same set of factors will lead to the same outcome next time they occur.

The concept of SOC forces us to distinguish cause and reason carefully: the single grain of sand can be the cause of an avalanche, but it is not the reason why avalanches take place. Steepness of the slope of the pile, adhesive forces between grains of sand and structural characteristics of the pile are all important reasons for the kind of adjustments that avalanches are. The final grain of sand triggers the avalanche. Likewise, a set of psycholinguistic (such as availability of elements) and sociolinguistic factors (such as being in a setting in which CS is the conversational norm) make people switch code, but they do not necessarily define why a particular CS takes place at a given moment and what form it takes. It should be pointed out here that the language system of a bilingual is always in a critical state: depending on the setting, only one of the languages may be used, but in settings in which CS is either the norm or there are no restrictions on the use of more than one language, the systems will move into a state in which a switch is about to take place. Various factors may interact to make a language system critical and very sensitive to minor changes that might lead to a phase change or code switch. There may be many phenomena that trigger a CS. Given the critical state of the system a minor change in one of its subsystems may cause a switch to a smaller or larger chunk in the other language. A sound from the other language, the thought of an event specific to a particular language setting, the occurrence of a word, sound, gesture or construction from the other language may be enough to make the system switch and in this sense lead to a change of state of the system. In other words, the grain of sand is analogous to the trigger and the switch to an avalanche. The specific configuration of interacting variables will be very idiosyncratic: all the individual's experiences are reflected in her present state, and what may be a trigger for one individual may have no effect at all for another individual.

In physics there is a world of research on phase transformations, such as the change of ice into water or gas into a fluid state. A change of the language system that leads to a switch can be seen as a state phase transition from $L_a$ to $L_b$. Triggering can have the effect that at all levels or just on a minor local level the system changes phase. Following ideas on SOC, the impact from a specific trigger can not be predicted, but the effects are assumed to follow a power law function which states that over longer periods of time and many iterations, there will be many small changes, and a small number of larger ones. The essence of this line of thinking is that the larger ones are not simply outliers, but part of a normal pattern and therefore do not need a special explanation. Or, to use the common terminology for this, they follow a power law.

Criticality plays an important role in CDST models in various disciplines. So far it has not been applied to language. It presents a useful model for specific types of CS. The model as presented leads to smooth switches that are internally generated. So, following this model, it does not imply the complete activation of one language and the complete deactivation of another one. Languages just differ slightly in activation, which makes switching light.

In this section I have tried to show that some of the core concepts of CDST, the criticality of systems, also applies to aspects of language use, exemplified here with respect to CS. It could be argued that the notion of "restructuring" (McLaughlin 1990) is an example of SOC. In her discussion of this concept, Lightbown (1985: 17) already linked ideas of CDST and criticality with restructuring in language learning:

> Restructuring occurs, because language is a complex hierarchical system whose components interact in non-linear ways. Seen in these terms, an increase in error rate in one area may reflect an increase in complexity or accuracy in another, followed by overgeneralization of a newly acquired structure, or simply by a sort of overload of complexity which forces a restructuring, or at least a simplification in another part of the system.

## 8.5 The analysis of language variation

Inter-individual and intra-individual variation are typical in the process of language development. Variability is seen as a necessary condition for development to take place. "It is a basic tenet of CDST that for change to occur, stable patterns must become unstable in the endogenous environment of the learner in order to allow the learner's system to self-organize in new ways" (Larsen-Freeman and Cameron 2008: 122). In the sociolinguistic approach to variation, the factors looked at (age, level of education, SES) are typically treated as fixed and static variables. In development, variation is often assessed by comparing individuals' data with group data and in particular with native speakers of a language. Variation in that perspective is basically a deviation from the norm. CDST radically rejects the automatic retreat to such an error hypothesis and claims that variability bears important information about the nature of the developmental process. CDST stresses the importance of the context in which the behavior is displayed. Development takes place in real time and is considered highly context dependent. Therefore, it can be compared with an evolutionary process, which is also mindless and opportunistic. Thelen and Smith agree with the classical Darwinian emphasis on variability as the source of new forms. They state: "We believe that in development, as in evolution, change consists of successive make-do solutions that work, given abilities, goals and history of the organisms at the time" (1994: 144). Variability is considered to be the result of the systems' flexibility and adaptability to the environment. From a dynamic systems angle, variability has been viewed as both the source of development and the indicator of a specific moment in the developmental process, namely in the presence of a developmental transition (Van Dijk 2003: 129).

Intrinsic to this view is the idea that individual developmental paths, each with all its variation, may be quite different from one another, even though in a "grand sweep" view these developmental paths are quite similar. While the statistics of the true score approach are well developed and offer researchers the comfort of clear demarcations of what is "significant" and what is not (or so it seems), methods to look at variation as a source of information from a CDST perspective are only beginning to be developed (see Van Dijk and Van Geert (2005) for several interesting techniques).

Larsen-Freeman (2006) reports on a study in which the oral and written production of five Chinese learners of English is examined. The data show "the mergence of complexity, fluency, and accuracy ... not as the unfolding of some prearranged plan, but rather as a system adapting to a changing context, in which the language resources of each individual are uniquely transformed through use" (590). These data support Larsen-Freeman's earlier statement that a CDST perspective

> rejects a view of language as something that is taken in – a static commodity that one acquires and therefore possesses forever. In its place, a complex system view suggests that development is always happening and there is no finite state at which it ceases.
>
> (2006: 585)

Spoelman and Verspoor (2010) studied the development of a learner of Finnish as a foreign language using her written assignments over her period of study. The study focused on intra-individual variability in accuracy rates and complexity measures. The study demonstrates several useful CDST methods and techniques to measure variability, including min-max graphs and Monte Carlo analyses to elucidate significance in such variability. Word complexity and sentence complexity develop simultaneously and can be seen as "connected growers".

Chan (2015) reports on a CDST study with identical twins in Taiwan who wrote short pieces of text in English every week over a period of eight months. The data show that even though the twins were monozygotic and raised in a similar environment, there were considerable differences between them over time on a number of aspects. The dynamic correlations of two types of lexical complexity were described through a mathematical model (the hidden Markov model), and the directions of the relations between writing and speaking were not similar among the identical twins.

## 8.6 Individual differences and CDST

Maybe the area in AL in which CDST is having the strongest impact is individual differences, and in particular in the study of attitudes and motivation. In the last decade a number of researchers, including Zoltán Dörnyei, Peter MacIntyre, Kimberley Noels and Emma Ushioda, have systematically explored the potential for CDST in the study of motivation. Dörnyei (2014) provides a sketch of the challenges of motivation research since the early work of Gardner and Lambert in the late 1950s. He shows how the static and linear approach to motivation proposed by these authors held sway for many years but was ultimately overcome by the move to a micro-perspective on motivation that did not treat motivation as a factor that was statically assessed using surveys. The analyses at the micro level showed the complexity, interconnectedness and messiness of motivational forces at the individual level.

Early signs of the growing interest in CDST in research on motivation can be found in Dörnyei and Skehan:

> During the lengthy process of mastering certain subject matters, motivation does not remain constant, but is associated with a dynamically changing and evolving process, characterized by constant (re)appraisal and balancing of the various internal and external influences that the individual is exposed to. Indeed, even within the duration of a single course of instruction, most learners experience a fluctuation of their enthusiasm/commitment, sometimes on a day-to-day basis.
>
> (2003: 617)

Dörnyei (2014) argues that three initiatives cleared the way for a non-linear systems approach to SLD: emergentism (e.g. Ellis and Larsen-Freeman 2006), Dynamic Systems Theory (e.g. de Bot *et al.* 2007) and Complexity Theory (Larsen-Freeman and Cameron 2008). These converging strands led to a new perspective on motivation. "Motivation is less a trait than fluid play, an ever-changing one that emerges from the processes of interaction of many agents, internal and external, in the ever-changing complex world of the learner" (Ellis and Larsen-Freeman 2006: 563). This complex interaction is beautifully phrased by Lewis *et al.*:

> In conceptualizing the relationship between emotion and cognition neither should be described as causing the other; rather, each continually and progressively chases the other, weaving separate threads of behavior into a single composition, a fugue.
>
> (1984: 285–6)

This close link between emotion and cognition is also foregrounded in Verspoor's (2014) reference to Edelman's work on the conceptualization of action/perception/evaluation as the driving force in development. Iterative steps are evaluated and that evaluation sparks the iterative process, it provides the feedback that gives direction.

The changing views on development and motivation also lead to a reformulation of research questions. MacIntyre (2014) suggests how traditional questions with respect to motivation, willingness to communicate and language anxiety can be rephrased in CDST terms. Some of the changes he proposes are listed in Table 8.1.

He points out that "rephrasing these questions allows us to observe the intra-individual variation of numerous processes that co-occur on a timescale of seconds and minutes" (MacIntyre 2014, conference handout). For the standard research questions correlational studies based on surveys or introspective methods are used and these provide "clear" outcomes, such as correlations between 0.30 and 0.60 between anxiety and course grades. But the CDST research questions dig deeper and call for data on finer timescales. What exactly the relationship between physical arousal measures and mental states is, is less clear, but the data make it clear in a fairly direct way that cognition is embodied: changes in mental states correlate significantly with reported states of stress or positive feelings.

The new questions that arise from a CDST perspective call for other methods of research that allow us to look at variation at different timescales.

*Table 8.1* Standard versus CDST research questions

| Standard research question | CDST research question |
| --- | --- |
| Does anxiety correlate with course grades? | What happens when anxiety rises during a test? |
| Are extraverts more willing to communicate? | At the moment of choice, what are extraverts thinking? |
| Does motivation predict proficiency? | What happens to word choice as avoidance motivation rises? |

Ideally, we would like to measure changes on a range of timescales ranging from seconds to years. MacIntyre developed a set of measures based on physiological indicators, such as skin resistance and heart rate, that appear to vary with variables like anxiety and willingness to communicate. By combining the physiological indicators with post-hoc viewing of the session with the participant he was able to link spikes in the signals with emotional events. This method provides many data points, so allowing for advanced statistical analyses.

Most of the recent research on motivation uses the CDST perspective to gather and analyze data. There are some attempts to move to more quantitative data, but these are still being developed. In 2014, Dörnyei *et al.* published an anthology with research papers that had been carefully selected for CDST methodology and concepts. In the same year, they organized an international conference on the dynamics of motivation that attracted some 175 participants from 30 different countries, which points to the growth of the dynamic turn in research on motivation.

## 8.7 CDST and timescales

Dynamics is about change over time. But time is not easily defined. While in daily language use we have, buy, lose and win time, we have no organ to measure the passing of time. "In so far as time is something different from events, we do not perceive time as such, but changes or events in time" (Le Poidevin 2010: 1). The timescales we use in our studies of developmental processes define what we will see.

> The grand sweep of development seems neatly rule-driven. In detail, however, development is messy. As we turn up the magnification of our microscope, we see that our visions of linearity, uniformity, inevitable sequencing and even irreversibility break down. What looks like a cohesive, orchestrated process from afar takes on the flavor of a more exploratory, opportunistic, syncretic and function-driven process in its instantiation.
>
> (Thelen and Smith 1994: xvi)

We can look at events at different timescales from the millisecond to the life span. No timescale is absolute, since there is no absolute stable reference, so time is dynamic rather than static.

In a CDST perspective, what we observe is defined by the timescales we use to gather data. Each timescale has its own unique picture of events. Timescales interact, so what happens on the timescale of days has an impact on what happens on the hours or week scales. This adds to the complexity of phenomena. Not only do various factors defining it play a role in the development over time, but these factors all have an impact on their own timescale. An example could be the development of motivation over time

(Waninge *et al.* 2014). For language learning a student may be motivated at the year scale because she wants a good job for which knowledge of that language is mandatory. On the months scale she may be motivated by the prospect of the end of year examinations. On the week scale it may be the tests she has to do and on the day scale it may have to do with interactions with the teacher. The factors on these timescales interact and so form a CDS.

In research on CDST a distinction has been made between dynamical systems and dynamic systems. The former refer to the quantitative and mathematical approach to CDST, while the latter is oriented more on the qualitative and social aspect of CDST. The application of the mathematical tools of dynamical systems theory requires large numbers of data points. For instance, Van Orden *et al.* (2003) had informants repeat the same word 1,100 times in order to have enough power for the fractal analysis. For most of the research in AL such numbers are hard to reach.

One of the key concepts in CDST is the fractal nature of many processes that develop over time. The concept of fractals was developed by Mandelbrot. It refers to the self-similarity of phenomena at different scales of granularity. A fractal is "a rough or fragmented geometric shape that can be split into parts, each of which is (at least approximately) a reduced-size copy of the whole" (Mandelbrot 1982: 23). The best-known example of fractals is the shape of the coast of Britain that Mandelbrot pointed to. By changing the unit of analysis or the scale of measurement shapes are found that are similar at different grades of granularity.

Development can also be fractal in nature with similar patterns at different timescales. For the study of motivation fractals are interesting, since we may assume that there is similarity in patterns on different timescales (days/weeks/months). "In dynamic terms, the timescales may be fractal, or have self similarity at many levels of observation" (Thelen and Smith 1998: 277). But for a mathematical approach to fractals, very large numbers of data points are needed, which is problematic for measuring motivation, since we cannot measure levels of motivation on finer timescales (minutes/hours). There is a risk that such frequent assessments actually have an impact on the phenomena they intend to measure, because subjects will object to being asked to reveal their motivation so frequently. An interesting alternative is the use of physiological measures that are related to emotions. MacIntyre (2014) studied a group of learners of French in Canada and gathered online physiological data (event-related skin resistance and heart rate) while subjects carried out certain verbal tasks in their L2. After they had completed the task, the subjects were asked to reflect on the patterns the measurements revealed. For instance, when there was a spike in the physiological data, the subjects were asked what might have caused that change. Quite often the subjects reported word-finding problems at these moments. So this technique allows for registering changes in emotional state at the millisecond level with reflections on the minute level.

As mentioned at the beginning of the section, research on motivation and related phenomena such as language anxiety and willingness to communicate has been redefined in terms of CDST and this movement seems to have real momentum, probably more than in any other area of AL research. It shows that for paradigm shifts to happen, a strong commitment of leading researchers is needed. It is obvious that without the constant involvement and stimulation by Zoltán Dörnyei and Peter MacIntyre, the dynamic turn had not been as complete for this area of research as it is now.

## 8.8 Concluding remarks

In this chapter arguments have been provided to show that the dynamic turn can be seen as a paradigm shift in that some of the basic assumptions of the current information processing approach to cognition are untenable from a CDST perspective. This has to do with characteristics such as modularity, static representations and the relevance of isolated linguistic units for our understanding of what constitutes language as a tool for communication and a part of the cognitive system. Taking away these fundamentals of the information processing approach leads to far-reaching changes in theoretical orientation and research methodology. The interconnectedness of sub-systems calls for an integrative approach to empirical studies taking into account as many factors as possible without getting some vague wholeness that is impervious to empirical research.

A number of research topics that may be influenced by the CDST approach have been presented, including an analysis of the basic tenets of existing language processing models, the study of CS as an example of criticality of systems, variation in language development and the study of individual differences, in particular motivation. For all of these topics taking a CDST perspective leads to a fundamental reassessment of the basics of research. There are no doubt many other aspects of AL for which a CDST approach might be relevant.

## Notes

1 An earlier version of this section appeared in de Bot (2010).
2 This section is based on:
   de Bot, K., Broersma, M. and Isurin, L. (2009) "Sources of triggering in code switching" in: L. Isurin, D. Winford and K. de Bot (eds), *Multidisciplinary Approaches to Code-Switching*, Amsterdam: John Benjamins, pp. 103–20.

## References

Bak, P. (1996) *How Nature Works: The Science of Self-organized Criticality*, New York: Copernicus.
Bak, P., Tang, C. and Wiesenfeld, K. (1987) "Self-organized criticality: An explanation of 1/f noise", *Physical Review Letters*, vol. 59: 364.

Chan, H. (2015) "A dynamic approach to the development of lexicon and syntax in a second language", PhD, University of Groningen.

de Bot, K. (2004) "The multilingual lexicon: Modeling selection and control", *International Journal of Multilingualism*, vol. 1, no. 1: 17–32.

de Bot, K. (2010) "Cognitive processing in bilinguals: From static to dynamic models" in: R. Kaplan (ed.) *Oxford Handbook of Applied Linguistics*, Oxford: Oxford University Press, pp. 335–48.

de Bot, K. and Lowie, W. (2010) "On the stability of representations in the multilingual lexicon" in: L. Sicora (ed.), *Cognitive Processing in Second Language Acquisition*, Amsterdam: John Benjamins, pp. 117–34.

de Bot, K., Lowie, W. and Verspoor, M. (2005) *Second Language Acquisition: An Advanced Resource Book*, London: Routledge.

de Bot, K., Lowie, W. and Verspoor, M. (2007) "A dynamic view as a complementary perspective", *Bilingualism, Language and Cognition*, vol. 10, no. 1: 51–5.

Dörnyei, Z. (2009) *The Psychology of Second Language Acquisition*, Oxford: Oxford University Press.

Dörnyei, Z. (2014) "The challenges of motivation research in a dynamic world", keynote address, International Conference on Motivational Dynamics and Second Language Acquisition. Nottingham, 28–30 August.

Dörnyei, Z. and Skehan, P. (2003) "Individual differences in second language learning" in: C. Doughty and M. Long (eds), *The Handbook of Second Language Acquisition*, Oxford: Blackwell, pp. 589–630.

Eisner, F. and McQueen, J. (2006) "Perceptual learning in speech: Stability over time", *JASA*, vol. 4: 1950–3.

Ellis, N. and Larsen-Freeman, D. (2006) "Language emergence: Implications for applied linguistics", *Applied Linguistics*, vol. 27, no. 4: 558–89.

Elman, J. (2005) "Connectionist models of cognitive development: Where next", *Trends in Cognitive Sciences*, vol. 9, no. 3: 111–17.

Green, D. (1993) "Towards a model of L2 comprehension and production" in: B. Weltens (ed.), *The Bilingual Lexicon*, Amsterdam: Benjamins, pp. 249–78.

Hald, L., Bastiaanse, M. and Hagoort, P. (2006) "EEG theta and gamma responses to semantic violations in online sentence processing", *Brain and Language*, vol. 96, no. 1: 90–105.

Larsen-Freeman, D. (1997) "Chaos/complexity science and second language acquisition", *Applied Linguistics*, vol. 18, no. 2: 141–65.

Larsen-Freeman, D. (2006) "The emergence of complexity, fluency and accuracy in the oral and written production of five Chinese learners of English", *Applied Linguistics*, vol. 27: 590–619.

Larsen-Freeman, D. (2009) "Adjusting expectations: The study of complexity, accuracy, and fluency in second language acquisition", *Applied Linguistics*, vol. 30, no. 4: 579–89.

Larsen-Freeman, D. and Cameron, L. (2008) *Complex Systems and Applied Linguistics*, Oxford: Oxford University Press.

Le Poidevin, R. (2010) "Time without change (in three steps)", *American Philosophical Quarterly*, vol. 47: 171–80.

Lewis, M., Sullivan, M. and Michalson, L. (1984) "The cognitive-emotional fugue" in: C. Izard, J. Kagan and R. Zajonc (eds), *Emotions, Cognition and Behavior*, Cambridge: Cambridge University Press, pp. 264–88.

Lightbown, P. (1985) "Great expectations: Second language acquisition research and classroom teaching", *Applied Linguistics*, vol. 6: 173–89.

Lowie, W. and Verspoor, M. (2011) "The dynamics of multilingualism: Levelt's Speaking model revisited" in: M.S. Schmid and W. Lowie (eds), *From Structure to Chaos*, Amsterdam: John Benjamins, pp. 267–88.

MacIntyre, P. (2014) "Motivation, anxiety and willingness to communicate: New questions and new answers from a dynamic systems perspective", paper presented at International Conference on Motivational Acquisition and Second Language Acquisition. Nottingham, 28–30 August.

McLaughlin, B. (1990) "Restructuring", *Applied Linguistics*, vol. 11: 113–28.

Mandelbrot, B. (1982) *The Fractal Geometry of Nature*, New York: W.H. Freeman.

Nieuwland, M. and van Berkum, J. (2006) "When peanuts fall in love: N400 evidence for the power of discourse", *Journal of Cognitive Neuroscience*, vol. 18, no. 7: 1098–111.

Pickering, M. and Garrod, S. (2004) "Toward a mechanistic psychology of dialogue", *Behavioral and Brain Sciences*, vol. 27: 169–90.

Salomon, G. (1993) "Editor's introduction" in: G. Salomon (ed.), *Distributed Cognitions: Psychological and Educational Considerations*, Cambridge: Cambridge University Press, pp. ix–xxi.

Sankoff, D. (1998) "A formal production-based explanation of the facts of code switching", *Bilingualism, Language and Cognition*, vol. 1: 39–50.

Spivey, M. (2007) *The Continuity of Mind*, Oxford: Oxford University Press.

Spoelman, M. and Verspoor, M. (2010) "Dynamic patterns in development of accuracy and complexity: A longitudinal case study in the acquisition of Finnish", *Applied Linguistics*, vol. 31, no. 4: 532–53.

Thelen, E. and Smith, L.B. (1994) *A Dynamic Systems Approach to the Development of Cognition and Action*, Cambridge, MA: MIT Press.

Thelen, E. and Smith, L.B. (1998) "Dynamic systems theory" in: W. Damon and R. Bidell (eds), *Dynamic Development of Psychological Structures in Action and Thought*, New York: Wiley, pp. 258–312.

van Dijk, M. (2003) *Child Language Cuts Capers: Variability and Ambiguity in Early Child Development*, University of Groningen.

van Dijk, M. and van Geert, P. (2005) "Disentangling behavior in early child development: Interpretability of early child language and the problem of filler syllables and growing utterance length", *Infant Behavior and Development*, vol. 28: 99–117.

van Gelder, T. (1998) "The dynamical hypothesis in cognitive science", *Behavioral and Brain Sciences*, vol. 21: 615–56.

van Orden, G., Holden, J. and Turvey, M. (2003) "Self-organisation of cognitive performance", *Journal of Experimental Psychology: General*, vol. 132, no. 3: 331–50.

Verspoor, M. (2014) "Initial conditions: Variable or stable?", presentation International Conference on Motivational Dynamics and Second Language Acquisition. Nottingham, 28–30 August.

Verspoor, M., Lowie, W. and de Bot, K. (2011) *A Dynamic Approach to Second Language Development: Methods and Techniques*, Amsterdam and Philadelphia: John Benjamins.

Waninge, F., Doerniye, Z. and de Bot, K. (2014) "Motivational dynamics in language learning: Change, stability and context", *Modern Language Journal*, vol. 98, no. 3: 704–23.

# 9   The citation game

Traditionally, AL has been on the edge of the humanities and the social sciences, leaning more toward the latter than the former in recent times. This means that many of the developments in those areas have had an impact on AL. One fairly recent one is the role of publications and citations. Citations have, despite the warnings of people like Eugene Garfield, the godfather of the citation index, become all-important and can make or break an academic career.

Citation analysis is a new development in the 30 years covered in this study. Though Eugene Garfield's Institute for Scientific Information (ISI) was established in 1960, the Arts & Humanities Citation Index (AHCI) started only in 1975, and there are very few publications in the early 1980s attracting larger numbers of citations, so for the earlier decade citations are clearly not that relevant to measure impact.

This chapter is different from the other ones, as it is not based on my participants' views, but on their publications. I decided to add this chapter because analyses of citations provide a picture of the field that is hard to obtain through other data. It helps to show whether the people that are seen as leaders are also the ones cited most and it allows to a certain extent a comparison between disciplines. In this chapter, I will discuss the findings of a citation analysis of the informants in this study, how citations and impact scores are related to scores on leadership, and what the impact is of the most important AL journals.

The data for this analysis have mainly been gathered in January and February 2014, so there will be publications from after 2010. There is no way to retrospectively assess the citation scores on December 31, 2009. Even over a short period of time citation scores may change substantially, so the data used here are a snapshot of the field at one moment in time. Subsequent data collection and analysis will have to be done to assess the stability of the present findings.

## 9.1  Data sources for citation analysis

Citations are assumed to reflect the impact of a researcher (or a journal or a publisher) on the field. In order to be citable in bibliographic databases, a publication must be in a journal or book that is "seen" by the citation machine. There are basically two systems at the moment: Google Scholar (GS) and Web of Science (WoS). There seems to be a tendency, in particular for the humanities and social sciences, to use GS. Harzing (2011: 165) lists the following advantages of this system:

- It is free
- It is easy to use
- It is quick
- It is comprehensive in its coverage.

Access to WoS is costly: my university spends more than €120,000 a year on this package, and not all researchers in our field will be at institutions that have a subscription. GS is easy to use, without knowledge of underlying databases or bibliometric instruments. GS may be quick, but for more common names it will take minutes to find the citations and then the real work begins. For example, finding Alan Davies's h-index meant manually removing some 650 references. GS is comprehensive, it lists citations to books and book chapters, conference proceedings, working papers and government reports and, most importantly, journals not listed in the ISI database, that forms the basis for WoS, and journals in languages other than English.

Differences between the two systems can be huge. Batia Laufer's (2003) article in the *Canadian Modern Language Review* has a citation score of 28 in WoS and a score of 212 in GS. Similarly, her (2001) *Applied Linguistics* article, co-authored with Jan Hulstijn, has a citation score of 31 in WoS and 706 in GS. GS and WoS tend to have a different coverage for different fields of study. GS displays a better coverage for the social sciences and humanities while WoS works better for science and medicine (Kousha and Thelwall 2008).

There are, however, also problems with GS. The fact that GS is comprehensive also means that irrelevant or incorrect publications and citations are included. So-called "stray citations" are the most serious problem, but in WoS the same problem exists as well. Stray citations result from wrong spellings of names of publications or authors mainly. The comprehensiveness also means that publications that are not, or are seldom, cited will be included. An analysis of my own citations showed that out of 284 papers, 164 were either misspellings of other publications in the list, publications with less than three citations or other debris such as acknowledgements for reviewing in journals.[1] While such stray citations have no impact on the h-index, they do have an impact on indicators such as citations per publication.

For the present study the findings of Meho and Yang (2007) are relevant. They show that in particular for GS, coverage of publications before 1990 is incomplete, but this may have to do with the fact that publishers are still busy digitalizing older issues of journals and because things have probably improved since 2007. Still, there may be a bias for more recent publications. A 2008 comparison of WoS, Scopus, GS and PubMed concluded:

PubMed and Google Scholar are accessed for free … Scopus offers about 20 per cent more coverage than Web of Science, whereas Google Scholar offers results of inconsistent accuracy. PubMed remains an optimal tool in biomedical research. Scopus covers a wider journal range … but it is currently limited to recent articles (published after 1995) compared with Web of Science. Google Scholar, as for the web in general, can help in the retrieval of even the most obscure information but its use is marred by inadequate, less often updated, citation information.

(Falagas *et al.* 2008: 342)

## 9.2 Using Hirsch's h-index

There are different ways to measure a researcher's impact. Although ideally there would be many different indicators that assess the impact and quality of a publication, there is one indicator that has become more or less the standard in bibliometry; Hirsch's (2005) h-index, defined as:

A scientist has index h if h of his/her Np papers have at least h citations each, and the other (Np-h) papers have no more than h citations each.

In other words: a researcher has an h-index of 15 if 15 of her publications have been cited at least 15 times.

There are a number of variants of the h-index that remedy some of the disadvantages of this index, such as its age-relatedness. Some authors will continue to "harvest" an increasing h-index even when they have stopped publishing, since their earlier publications continue to be cited. An example in our database is Eric Kellerman, who produced a number of publications that are still cited, even though he switched fields from AL to professional photography and his most recent publication dates from 1997. Another disadvantage is that the h-index of a researcher can never go down. This can to a certain extent be remedied by looking at specific windows of time, e.g. total/last ten years/last five years.

For the current project it was decided to use the h-index as one of the indicators of impact. To calculate the h-indices, two citation analysis systems have been used: Google Scholar Citations (http://scholar.google.com) and Harzing's Publish or Perish (www.harzing.com). For GS the h-index can be found easily when a researcher has a profile in Scholar. For example, Batia Laufer's profile, as presented in Table 9.1 and Figure 9.1, shows her indicators (h and i10) in total and since 2009, and the development of her citations over time. Her profile page shows the list of her publications with the number of citations per publication. The i10 index is the number of publications that have been cited at least ten times. This indicator will not be used further in the analyses.

*Table 9.1* Batia Laufer's citation indices from Google Scholar

|  | All | Since 2009 |
|---|---|---|
| Citations | 8634 | 4922 |
| h-index | 42 | 35 |
| i10-index | 69 | 59 |

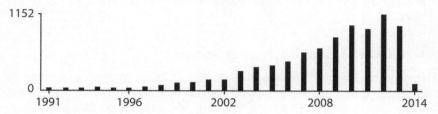

*Figure 9.1* Laufer (2003) citations over time

Not all the applied linguists in my database had set up such a profile, so another program was needed to assess the h-indices. For this Harzing's Publish or Perish (PoP) was used. Harzing (2011) is the handbook that goes with the program and that discusses the many types of indicators available with their pros and cons in detail.

Table 9.2 presents the outcomes of Batia Laufer's citation pattern according to PoP.

PoP produces a large number of indicators, including the total number of papers, total number of citations, average number of citations per year, per paper, per author, papers per author, author per paper and variants of the h-index. While all of these indicators may be useful, the focus will be on the h-index. The profiles in GS seem to be quite accurate in listing the publications of a given author, but extracting the indicators in PoP is often more work and is sometimes impossible. While Jim Lantolf and Kathleen Bardovi-Harlig have more or less unique names, and therefore their names as search terms lead to few false hits, other people, like Andrew Cohen and Karen Johnson, are less fortunate in this respect. There are many Cohens and Johnsons active in academia and the search options for selecting authors on the basis of first names are limited. Searches with such names lead to thousands (actually, GS limits the number to 1000) of citations and it is in fact impossible to select only the citations we are interested in. For less common

*Table 9.2* Output of PoP for Batia Laufer

| Papers: | 114 | Papers/author: | 83.60 | h-index: | 42 | Query date: 2014-02-21 |
|---|---|---|---|---|---|---|
| Citations: | 8662 | Cites/year: | 227.95 | g.index: | 93 | Papers: 114 |
| Years: | 38 | Cites/auth/year: | 167.63 | hc-index: | 24 | Citations: 8662 |
| Cites/paper: | 75.98 | hI,annual: | 1.05 | hI,norm: | 40 | Years: 38 |
|  |  |  |  |  |  | Cites/year: 227.95 |

names there may still be considerable numbers of false hits, and the false hits have to be removed manually, with a definite risk of selecting wrong citations.

In Batia Laufer's case the h-index for GS is the same as for PoP, but there may be differences. According to Harzing (2011: 46) such differences are the result of differences in algorithms used by the two systems (advanced scholar search versus standard scholar search). When there was a difference in h-indices between PoP and GS, the highest was used in the analyses of the present project.

## 9.3  Number of citations as an indicator

The h-index does not provide information on how often a publication has been cited. Some researchers have one or two very frequently cited publications and a larger series of less frequently cited ones. Examples in our database are Patsy Lightbown and Nina Spada, who have a very high citation score for their widely used book *How Languages are Learned* but lower ones for subsequent publications. The same holds for Rosamond Mitchell and Florence Myles and their book on theories of second language acquisition. For such books, that have seen various editions over time, the total number of citations is used, irrespective of the edition. In order to do justice to those frequently cited publications, I decided to include for each author the sum of the citation scores of the three most cited publications.

## 9.4  A database of applied linguists and their citations

An Excel database was set up in which the h-index and the citation scores for the three most cited publications were included for the 98 applied linguists of whom these data could be used in this study. In addition, for each of these publications information was added on when it was published, whether it was single- or multi-authored, a journal article, book chapter or book, and whether it was an overview study or a data based study.

The database allowed me to find answers to the following questions:

- How are the citations distributed over time?
- Are there differences in terms of citations between journal articles, book chapters and books?
- Are there differences in terms of citations between overview studies versus data based studies?
- Are there differences in terms of citation between single-authored publications and multi-authored publications?

The main statistics for the h-indices and number citations are summarized in Table 9.3.

The data in Table 9.3 show that there is substantial variation in both the h-values and total citations. The h-values show a normal distribution with

Table 9.3 Descriptives for h-value and total number of citations

|  | *h-value* | *Total citations* |
|---|---|---|
| N | 98 | 98 |
| Mean | 30.08 | 2472 |
| Median | 29.5 | 1430 |
| Mode | 15 (multiple, smallest value) | 125 (multiple, smallest value) |
| Standard deviation | 13.38 | 3539 |
| Range | 66 | 21271 |
| Minimum | 7 | 125 |
| Maximum | 73 | 21396 |

kurtosis and skewness < 1. The distribution of the totals of citations is not normally distributed, but right skewed with kurtosis = 14.7 and skewness = 3.6. The data show that there are a small number of informants with very large numbers of citations and many with less than 2000 citations, so the distribution more or less follows a power law.

For the two indicators, rank orders of the highest h-index and most frequently cited applied linguists could be established. Table 9.4 presents the rank orders of the 25 applied linguists with the highest h-index and the rank order of the 25 most frequently cited applied linguists. Data for all the applied linguists participating in this study are presented in Appendix 3.

In these tables books and articles are put together, but as we will see later on, books attract more citations, so ideally the data should be corrected for this. The two tables show that the two indicators used to assess impact are both relevant. Not surprisingly, the correlations between the h-indices and total number of citations are high (Spearman's $r_s$ = 0.795; $p$ < 0.001). Overall, high h-indices go with large numbers of citations, because that is what the h-index is based on. But there are clear differences. Some researchers have a high citation score and relatively small numbers of citations, for example Kathleen Bardovi-Harlig and Nick Ellis. The reverse also occurs, for example Dick Schmidt and Nina Spada. The correlation between h-index and the most frequently cited article is 0.69, so the added value of the second and third publication is rather small.

## 9.5 The impact of publications over time

When we publish an article, we hope that other researchers will pick it up quickly and cite it. Unfortunately, that does not seem to be the way things go. As examples I have analyzed two articles that have been cited more than a thousand times: Norris and Ortega's 2000 article and Firth and Wagner's 1997 article. Figures 9.2 and 9.3 present the citations over time of both articles.

A few interesting observations can be made from these figures. One is that these publications were already cited before they were published. For

*Table* 9.4 Applied linguists 1–25 on the basis of h-index and sum of three most frequently cited publications

| Top 25 according to h-Index | | | Top 25 according to total citations | | |
|---|---|---|---|---|---|
| Name | h-Index | citations | Name | h-Index | citations |
| Ellis, R. | 73 | 16,938 | Krashen | 62 | 21,396 |
| Long | 68 | 5,117 | Crystal | 61 | 18,958 |
| Oxford | 65 | 8,041 | Ellis, R. | 73 | 16,938 |
| Swain | 65 | 10,940 | Swain | 65 | 10,940 |
| Krashen | 62 | 21,396 | Bachman | 36 | 8,128 |
| Crystal | 61 | 18,958 | Oxford | 65 | 8,041 |
| Ellis, N. | 54 | 1,801 | Schmidt | 29 | 6,943 |
| Genesee | 54 | 2,194 | Widdowson | 47 | 6,168 |
| Dörnyei | 53 | 3,595 | Kramsch | 48 | 5,490 |
| Gass | 53 | 4,110 | Larsen-Freeman | 38 | 5,270 |
| Kramsch | 48 | 5,490 | Long | 68 | 5,117 |
| Widdowson | 47 | 6,168 | Pennycook | 45 | 4,340 |
| White | 46 | 2,434 | Lightbown | 35 | 4,320 |
| Nation | 45 | 3,697 | Spada | 28 | 4,248 |
| Pennycook | 45 | 4,340 | Gass | 53 | 4,110 |
| Laufer | 42 | 1,960 | Cook | 38 | 3,824 |
| Pavlenko | 42 | 1,560 | Nation | 45 | 3,697 |
| Tarone | 40 | 1,699 | Dörnyei | 53 | 3,595 |
| Bardovi-Harlig | 39 | 1,172 | Cohen | 34 | 3,410 |
| Cook | 38 | 3,824 | Candlin | 33 | 3,091 |
| Lantolf | 38 | 2,868 | Skutnabb-Kangas | 37 | 2,881 |
| Larsen-Freeman | 38 | 5,270 | Lantolf | 38 | 2,868 |
| Meara | 38 | 1,001 | Grabe | 33 | 2,708 |
| Spolsky | 38 | 2,331 | Rampton | 32 | 2,474 |
| Skutnabb-Kangas | 37 | 2,881 | White | 46 | 2,434 |

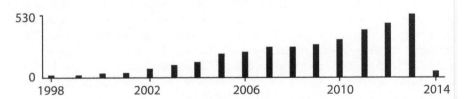

*Figure* 9.2 Norris and Ortega (2000) citations over time

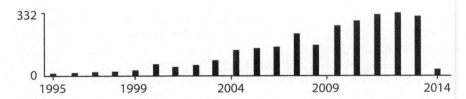

*Figure* 9.3 Firth and Wagner (1997) citations over time

example Norris and Ortega are cited in an article in *Applied Linguistics* by Lightbown in 2000. Given the production time of articles that means that she had access to this article in 1998. This is of course not uncommon; earlier versions of articles are typically circulated and referred to.

Another interesting aspect is the time it takes for an article to "take off". The number of citations per year is low in the first 5–7 years and the articles take close to 15 years to reach their full potential. This may also reflect the overall growth of the number of publications over this period: with a larger number of publications the chance of being cited increases too.

Related to the impact over time is the problem that some journals built up backlogs that led to substantial delays in the publication of articles, sometimes up to two years. In recent years more and more journals have made articles that are still to be published available through their website, which is useful for the field but a nightmare to the bibliometrist, who has to define when a paper was published. Is it the moment the article was available online or the moment it was published in the paper version of the journal? Long processing times can be a nuisance, in particular for PhDs whose dissertation consists of journal articles. Many graduate schools require that at least three articles in the dissertation have been formally accepted and preferably published.

## 9.6 Factors influencing citation scores

As mentioned earlier, the data provided answers to a number of questions. Each question will be dealt with separately below.

• How are the citations distributed over time?

The frequency distributions of the citations over time were calculated. The correlation between the number of citations and the year of publication is not significant. The distribution shows a peak in the period between 1998 and 2002. As we have seen, publications take time to have an impact, so the later articles will also be more influential in the years to come. In addition, the median for the years of publication of this set is 1987, with the oldest publication from 1972 and the most recent from 2014, which is actually beyond the time span of this study, but the two cases are recent editions of older books, like Lightbown and Spada and Ellis. Two factors play a role here: in order to show that they are up to date, researchers will tend to include the latest publications on a topic, so there will be a recency effect. On the other hand, older publications have more time to attract citations. The former factor should lead to a bias toward recent publications, while the latter would lead to a bias for older publications. The normal distribution suggests that the two factors are more or less in balance. For publications from the 1970/1980s an additional problem is that you could only cite something if you had access to a physical copy of it, and that was no doubt a limiting factor in citations (Paul Meara p.c.).

- Are there differences in terms of citations between journal articles, book chapters and books?

There are 138 books, 134 articles and 22 book chapters in the list of publications with the highest number of citations. A comparison using Mann-Whitney U tests shows that books are cited more frequently than articles (*Mdn* books = 510, *Mdn* articles = 341, $U$ = 6550, $p$ < 0.001). No differences were found between chapter and books or chapters and articles, but that may also be caused by the small number of chapters mentioned.

- Are there differences in terms of citations between overview studies versus data based studies?

Of the 291 publications that could be classified, 70 are overview articles and 221 data-driven articles. Overview articles are cited somewhat more frequently (*Mdn* = 466) than data-driven articles (*Mdn* = 407), but the difference is not significant ($U$ = 7240, $p$ = 0.419). This may be partly due to the large difference in sample size.

- Are there differences in terms of citation between single-authored publications and multi-authored publications?

One of the factors that make it hard to compare impact between disciplines is the number of authors. In science and medicine five or more authors is quite normal. The list of most cited papers in the science-oriented open access journal *PLOS-ONE* contains no single-authored articles, and most of them have five or more authors. In AL there are few articles with more than three authors. In the analysis a distinction was made between single- and multi-authored, but multi is typically two or three. Of the 243 publications mentioned, 139 are single-authored and 104 multi-authored. Single-authored publications attract more citations (median = 513) than multi-authored publications (median = 384). This difference is significant ($U$ = 6163, $p$ = 0.049).

## 9.7 Leaders and citations

In order to find out to what extent there is a relationship between number of citations and leadership, the data on the number of times someone is mentioned as a leader from Table 4.1 in Chapter 4 have been combined with the citation scores. The correlation is significant (Spearman's $r_s = 0.44$; $p$ < 0.01), but not very high. Figure 9.4 shows the scattergram of the data.

The data show a clustering of informants, with relatively low scores on both indications and a few with rather low citation totals but higher listings as leaders. So leadership partly depends on academic status and impact, but other factors clearly play a role, too.

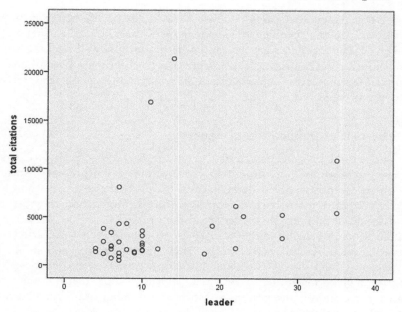

*Figure 9.4* Scattergram of leadership listings and total of citations

## 9.8 Cronyism, ignorism, Matthew effects and other dubious practices

I cite you and you cite me and we both cite our friend Harry. This behavior is not uncommon in any branch of science, as noted by Cole and Cole (1973) who coined the term "cronyism". Though in principle this is unethical if the reference would not have been included otherwise, it is typical of situations where there are competing groups in an area. High citation scores are always desirable to strengthen the common cause.

The opposite of cronyism could be called "ignorism"; not mentioning a publication because it is written by an "enemy", someone from a competing group, even though the publication would be relevant for the research reported on.

Less problematic, but distorting the idea of equal treatment, is a form of the Matthew effect: publications that already have a high citation score tend to attract more citations than publications that have a lower citation score.

Yet another strategy is to self-cite abundantly. It is not a very elegant strategy and researchers who overdo this lower their status among their peers. In particular university managers are very concerned about self-citations, since they may lead to higher impact factors than citations should indicate. But according to Harzing (2011: 183), "excluding self-citations is almost always a waste of time". Paul Meara suggests another strategy to lift citations: someone could review lots of manuscripts for journals, and insist that the papers he recommends should cite his own work. Related to this is the risk that papers that cite a reviewer's work may have a higher chance to be accepted. A final problematic tendency is "black boxing": using a large number of references to support a point. It shows how well read the author is and how strong the support is for her ideas or findings. Careful analysis readily shows that many references are only marginally or not at all relevant to the point made.

## 9.9 The risk of publication pressures

The publication pressure can lead to superficial reading and not checking original publications: Simkin and Roychowdhury (2003) present disturbing data on an estimation of the percentage of people that cite a paper and have actually read it. On the basis of copied misprint information they estimate that only about 20 percent of citers read the original.

Publication in a high-ranking journal is no guarantee that an article will actually be cited. An analysis of 225 journals in immunology and surgery by Weale *et al.* (2004) shows that some 23 percent of the articles in these journals from a given month never get cited. They also show that there is a high negative correlation between impact factors and number of non-cited articles. To what extent this also applies for AL journals is not clear.

## 9.10 AL journals and their impact

The informants were asked about the journals they use regularly. The original question was: "Which journals do you read?", but obviously in practice most researchers will not read journals cover to cover but do a search using GS, WoS or Scopus, which is likely to include articles from those journals. But the gist of the question remains the same and most informants listed the following journals in alphabetical order:

- *Applied Linguistics*
- *Bilingualism: Language and Cognition*
- *Language Learning*
- *Modern Language Journal*
- *Studies in Second Language Acquisition*
- *TESOL Quarterly.*

Other journals mentioned regularly are:

- *Annual Review of Applied Linguistics*
- *Applied Psycholinguistics*
- *Cognition*
- *International Journal of Applied Linguistics* (InJAL)
- *International Journal of Bilingualism*
- *International Review of Applied Linguistics* (IRAL)

- *Journal of Multilingual and Multicultural Development*
- *Journal of Second Language Writing*
- *Language Awareness*
- *Linguistic Approaches to Bilingualism*
- *Second Language Research*
- *Working Papers on Bilingualism.*

The journal impact factor is based on the average number of citations of articles in the journal in the previous two years. So the 2010 impact factor is calculated on the basis of the articles in the journal from 2008 and 2009. The 2010 impact factor is published in 2011, since all the 2010 articles have to be processed by the indexing agency. New journals, or existing journals that have been included recently in the set of referenced journals, will get an impact factor after two years of indexing. The journal impact factor has been criticized on the grounds that the distributions of the citations are not normally distributed, but follow a power law distribution, which means that there will be a few articles that attract the larger part of the citations and many articles that are hardly cited. For such, a distribution taking the arithmetic mean is statistically inappropriate. Therefore, direct comparisons of journals between disciplines on the basis of the impact factor are unwarranted. Ideally, the distributions of the citations should be added.

Table 9.5 presents the impact factors of the top six journals mentioned earlier. For the analysis use is made of the Journal Citation Report (JCR) function in WoS.

As the data in Table 9.5 show, not all journals have been indexed over the 1980–2010 period. *Bilingualism: Language and Cognition* only started in 1998, so there is no impact factor until 2000. The JCR function in WoS only gives impact factors from 1997 onwards.[2] There is quite some variation over time, but the trend does not seem to go in any specific direction. In contrast to the individual h-index, the impact factor of a journal can go down since it is based ultimately on the number of citations its articles attract. The mean for these six journals is 1.46 for 2012 and 1.57 for 2013, with a range of 1.00 for *TESOL Quarterly* to 2.05 for *Studies in Second Language Acquisition*. It should be mentioned here that compared to other disciplines, impact factors for AL journals tend to be low. The medical journal *Cell* has an impact factor of 31.9, the *Journal of Experimental Psychology: General* has an impact factor of 4.8. The impact factor reflects the number of researchers in a certain discipline and accordingly the number of publications and citations. AL is comparatively a small field.

## 9.11 More advanced analyses

In recent years, new methods for analyzing publication data have been developed. Meara has explored the possibilities of co-citation analyses. This method can be used to find out what central issues and central researchers

*Table 9.5* Impact factors of the top six AL journals 1995–2013

| Journal | AL | BLC | LL | SSLA | TQ | MLJ |
|---|---|---|---|---|---|---|
| 2013 | 1.833 | 1.907 | 1.433 | 2.051 | 1.000 | 1.181 |
| 2012 | 1.500 | 2.229 | 1.318 | 1.800 | 0.792 | 1.114 |
| 2011 | 1.885 | 1.714 | 1.218 | 1.111 | 0.969 | 1.299 |
| 2010 | 1.340 | 1.691 | 1.494 | 1.571 | 0.646 | 1.328 |
| 2009 | 1.469 | 1.636 | 0.984 | 1.323 | 0.942 | 1.914 |
| 2008 | 2.217 | 2.049 | 1.545 | 2.094 | 0.972 | 1.044 |
| 2007 | 1.178 | 0.756 | 0.417 | 1.485 | – | 0.793 |
| 2006 | 1.050 | – | 0.714 | 2.417 | 0.393 | 1.145 |
| 2005 | 1.029 | – | 0.976 | – | 0.700 | 1.188 |
| 2004 | 0.829 | – | 0.851 | – | – | 0.750 |
| 2003 | 1.026 | – | 0.680 | – | 1.000 | 0.438 |
| 2002 | 0.650 | – | 0.581 | – | 0.673 | 0.367 |
| 2001 | 0.795 | – | 0.682 | – | 0.508 | 1.042 |
| 2000 | 0.692 | – | 0.340 | – | 0.806 | 0.918 |
| 1999 | 0.590 | – | 0.410 | – | 0.938 | 0.882 |
| 1998 | 0.500 | – | 0.541 | – | 0.983 | 0.980 |
| 1997 | 0.889 | – | 0.385 | – | 1.391 | 0.765 |
| 1996 | 0.625 | | | | | |
| 1995 | 0.581 | | | | | |

are by looking at who is co-cited with whom. Meara (2012) looked at research literature on vocabulary acquisition in 2006. The analysis of 101 authors who were co-cited reveals that there were two clusters; a psycholinguistic one dominated by de Groot, Kroll and Green, and a mainstream vocabulary cluster dominated by Nation and Laufer. The data suggest that co-citation analysis may be useful to track changes in a discipline over time. Meara (2014) reports on a co-citation analysis of 201 articles on vocabulary acquisition that appeared in *The Modern Language Journal* between 1916 and 2010. The data from the earlier decades appeared to be hard to interpret since citation habits and journal article formats were different from present ones. But the analysis showed how the main research topics change over time, with sometimes little overlap between decades. More recent data (Meara p.c.) on changes over time in the journal *Applied Linguistics* provided additional evidence on changes in the field. Co-citation data may allow us to see what clusters there are in our field and then check to what extent the clusters found coincide with professional perceptions. This type of analysis may provide information on the leaders in the field and the possibility of finding different research areas with their own leaders. The data for co-citation are available in GS, but need to be adapted for the types of analysis Meara has done.

## 9.12 Conclusion

In this chapter information was provided on the use of citation analysis for publications in AL books and journals. Two measures have been used to assess the impact of researchers, their h-index and the sum of the number of citations of their three most cited publications. The data show that the h-indices are normally distributed, but the total numbers of citations seem to show more of a power law distribution, with a few authors or publications attracting large numbers of citations, such as Rod Ellis's (1994) 'The study of second language acquisition' reaching a impressive 9571 citations. The highest total number was found for Stephen Krashen (21,396). Rod Ellis had the highest h-index score (73).

To what extent the citation data reflect real impact as perceived by the field, becomes clear when the data on "leaders" are compared to the citation data. The correlation is moderately high: leaders have above average citation scores, though the interviews also show that the definition of leader is not uniform, as mentioned in Chapter 4. Clearly, academic status is an important component.

In contrast to Garfield's (1994) concern that editors of journals may prefer review articles because they attract more citations, the data show that there are only a few review studies that attract many citations. Numbers of citations for overview articles versus data-driven articles do not differ significantly.

In AL, we rarely find articles with more than three authors, and there seems to be a preference for single-authored publications. This is probably a remnant of the old humanities tradition, in which scholars worked on their own. This is in contrast to the situation in the hard sciences, where project based research is more common. The analyses showed, however, that single-authored publications are cited more frequently than multi-authored publications, but the difference is small and cannot lead to the conclusion that, in general, publishing in isolation is more effective.

When comparing publishing in books or journal articles, the question is whether, in terms of citation scores and h-indices, the investment in a whole book is warranted. It could be argued that the time investment for a book is roughly the same as for five journal articles. A simple calculation shows that books are not cited five times more often than articles.

Contrary to expectations, older publications are not cited more than more recent publications. The correlation between year of publication and number of citations is not significant. This is partly explained by the tendency to refer to more recent publications.

Over the last 15 years, impact factors of journals have become important in decisions on where to publish and on what counts. In the medical faculty of my university, researchers are encouraged to publish only in the top 25 percent journals of their specialization, and discouraged to publish in lower ranking journals, in the sense that their resources for research will increase with publications in the top 25 percent and decline with publications in the lowest quartile. This harsh regime does not seem to apply equally in AL, though the pressure to publish in good journals, often at the expense of publishing books, is mentioned frequently by the informants. As Robert DeKeyser remarked: "Impact factors may lead to undesirable publishing habits by both authors and journal editors." Editorial boards are keen on impact factors for their journals and editors may be tempted to go for pub-lications that are likely to attract citations rather than articles that have a high quality but are more mainstream.

Journal impact factors are beginning to play a role in our field. Of course, editors and editorial boards of journals keep an eye on impact factors, but the data show that there is some variation in scores over time, albeit not a clear trend. The tendency of journals to increase the number of issues per year to deal with the large number of submissions also leads, on the one hand, to more publications that could cite the articles of a given journal, since the total volume of articles increases. On the other hand, there could be a tendency toward a lowering of the number of citations per article, because there must be more articles that attract citations to have a high impact factor.

The importance of citations and impact factors is here to stay, despite all the criticism that has been voiced against it. To what extent high impact factors are a sign of the strength of a research community is a matter of debate. Indices have been shown to be manipulable and in that sense can never be the last word in important decisions. The pressure to publish in international peer-reviewed journals, typically the ones that will play a role in citation counts, has become stronger and the effects of this change have to be studied. Some argue that pressure to publish has led to too many second-class articles, and to the squeezing out of one set of data for as many publications as possible.

Finally, the work by Paul Meara on co-citation analysis may be very useful to get a better idea of the structure of the field, since it allows for analyses that show the clusters of researchers working on similar topics.

## Notes

1 Paul Meara (p.c.) adds: "Another problem with GS is that it tries to be compre-hensive, and this means that it includes a lot of rubbish publications – papers that appear in obscure journals that don't really make a contribution to the subject. These papers tend to cite the big names as a sort of automatic reflex (vocabulary: must cite Nation), and this means that the big names get more and more citations."

2 I am grateful to our librarian Michiel Thomas for helping me find these figures.

## References

Cole, J. and Cole, S. (1973) *Social Stratification in Science*, Chicago: University of Chicago Press.

Falagas, M., Pitsouni, E., Malietzis, G. and Pappas, G. (2008) "Comparison of PubMed, Scopus, Web of Science, and Google Scholar: Strengths and weaknesses", *FASEB Journal*, vol. 22, no. 2: 338–42.

Firth, A. and Wagner, J. (1997) "On discourse, communication and (some) fundamental concepts in SLA research", *The Modern Language Journal*, vol. 81, no. 3: 285–300.

Garfield, E. (1994) *The Thompson Reuters Impact Factor*, London: Thompson Reuters.

Harzing, A. (2011) *The Publish or Perish Book*, Melbourne: Tarma Software Research.

Hirsch, J. (2005) "An index to quantify an individual's scientific research output", *PNAS*, vol. 102, no. 46: 16569–72.

Kousha, K. and Thelwall, M. (2008) "Sources of Google Scholar citations outside the Science Citation Index: A comparison between four science disciplines", *Scientometrics*, vol. 74, no. 2: 273–94.

Laufer, B. (2003) "Vocabulary acquisition in a second language: Do learners acquire most vocabulary by reading?", *Canadian Modern Language Review*, vol. 59, no. 4: 567–85.

Laufer, B. and Hulstijn, J. (2001) "Incidental vocabulary acquisition in a second language: The construct of task-induced involvement", *Applied Linguistics*, vol. 22, no. 1: 1–26.

Meara, P. (2012) "The bibliometrics of vocabulary acquisition: An exploratory study", *RELC Journal*, vol. 43, no. 1: 7–22.

Meara, P. (2014) "Vocabulary research in the Modern Language Journal: A bibliometric analysis", *Vocabulary Learning and Instruction*, advance online publication.

Meho, L. and Yang, K. (2007) "A new era in citation and bibliometric analyses: Web of Science, Scopus and Google Scholar", *Journal of the American Society for Information Science and Technology*, vol. 58: 1–21.

Norris, J. and Ortega, L. (2000) "Effectiveness of L2 instruction: A research synthesis and quantitative meta-analysis", *Language Learning*, vol. 50, no. 3: 417–528.

Simkin, M. and Roychowdhury, V. (2003) "Read before you cite!", *Complex Systems*, vol. 14: 269–74.

Weale, A., Bailey, M. and Lear, P. (2004) "The level of non-citation of articles within a journal as a measure of quality: A comparison to the impact factor", *BMC Medical Research Methodology*, vol. 4: 1471.

# 10 The impact of applied linguistic research on language learning and teaching

In the early years of AL, the label was basically synonymous with language teaching and this continues to be a major part of what goes on in AL. There is probably not another topic on which views vary so much as on this one. The wording in the questionnaire was: "To what extent has AL research led to an improvement of language teaching and learning?" It is the question the informants indicate they found most difficult to answer. The reactions can globally be divided into six categories: I don't know/no application of research/research has a negative impact/no impact/some impact/considerable to huge impact. Some impact may refer to some impact on different aspects or to substantial impact on a limited set of aspects.

## 10.1 I don't know

Several people answered that they do not know. Martin Bygate:

> I feel totally unable to answer this question. I simply don't know. I believe that little has been done to investigate the impact of AL research on language education, and this is one reason why reading research in the field gives little or no basis for assessing the impact of AL on language education.

This is also more or less Karlfried Knapp's perception:

> To what extent and how AL research has had a positive effect on language education can hardly be assessed in general, given that education systems vary considerably across nations and that in many countries, such systems determine what and how much of new insights from AL may seep into official language policies, curricula, teaching materials and teacher education.

## 10.2 No application

Lydia White argues: "Research findings don't necessarily have direct applications." Along similar lines, Michael Sharwood Smith distinguishes research on SLA, which is theory oriented and does not have application as its main goal, and AL defined more broadly, which does have application of research findings as its goal. This view is also expressed by Aneta Pavlenko: "The best contribution AL research can make and continues to make is to basic science, in terms of highlighting the psycholinguistic mechanisms of second language acquisition and multilingualism and illuminating ways languages and multilingualism function in today's global society."

## 10.3 Negative impact

Celeste Kinginger states: "Krashen and the natural approach resulted in a net decline in the quality of language teaching in US universities, especially when paired with the rise of institutionalized online grammar instruction." Guy Cook is equally negative about the impact of research:

> I don't think it has. On the contrary, I think many movements, such as SLA, CLT (Communicative Language Teaching), TBLT (Task-based Language Teaching) have done a great deal of harm, by promoting Anglo centric native-speaker models to the detriment of more inclusive and bilingual approaches. However, "improvement" is a relative term. So what is regarded as "improvement" changes from decade to decade, as values change.

## 10.4 Little or no impact

Wolfgang Klein expresses his perception succinctly: "I see no evidence for a major improvement." Quite a few applied linguists share his views. Richard Young mentions his own recent experience with learning Chinese:

> I have recently begun to brush up my knowledge of Chinese. In doing so I have been unpleasantly surprised by the extent to which the textbook, the teaching methods, and the learning activities that my teacher is using in 2014 are similar to the ways in which I studied French and German as a teenager at school in London.

Andrew Cohen shares this view: "Teaching has maybe improved, but I still see an awful lot of traditional language teaching."

Jim Lantolf thinks that research has not had the impact it should have had. Teachers do not want to know about theories. He points to the difference between ESL teachers who seem to be more open to innovation and the teachers of foreign languages like German and French, who still use grammar books as the basis for their teaching. Johannes Wagner thinks the explanation for this goes back to the past:

> Due to historical reasons, the teaching of English has never been marred by the long history of grammar teaching, brought about by the inheritance

of Latin and Greek in the teaching of French and German. This has certainly been a blessing for the teaching of English. But I would strongly argue that it wasn't the great teachers of English, such as Jespersen and consorts in the direct method area which created the teaching of English in a different spirit, but the social changes and modernization to which the story of English has been knitted and which created a social environment in which Jespersen *et al.* could start from afresh.

I myself see a similar gradation: there first seems to be a tendency of innovation in second language teaching (Dutch/German/Swedish as a second language), then in EFL, and then in foreign language teaching. For Dutch, this has led to a disparity between Dutch taught abroad, which tends to be very traditional, and Dutch as a second language, which embraces new approaches more easily. Within foreign language teaching, EFL tends to be more innovative than French or German as a foreign language. Paul Meara sees a similar trend in the UK: "I think AL has influenced EFL teaching a lot, but, in the UK at least, it has had a minimal impact on foreign language teaching."

Thomas Ricento sees little impact:

> I think that research has tended to have limited application. For example, if you look at the articles in the *Focus on Form* book, edited by Doughty and Williams (1998), the various conclusions from the research is something like "some things we do in the classroom may make some small difference for some students in some contexts." That is about it. Good research, but of very limited practical usefulness in terms of teaching practices/pedagogy.

According to Jasone Cenoz, "the influence of AL on language education is limited because most research on AL can't be applied to language education programs". Says Alastair Pennycook: "Poor research, self-interest and too quick jumps into applications have often caused difficulties for language education, pulling it in different directions. It is not clear that SLA theory or approaches to methodology have helped language education." Barbara Seidlhofer even goes one step further by claiming that: "What we do is based on the assumption that we contribute to the effectiveness of teaching and learning, but basically we are doing things for ourselves."

Annick De Houwer:

> From my European perspective I haven't seen much improvement in language teaching. I have been training future EFL teachers, and it is still an uphill battle to counter the grammar-translation method and to do away with vocabulary list learning. Insights from AL are apparently not easily applicable! Also, rigid monolingual, standard norms continue to

exist, both in how linguistically diverse children at preschool are approached and in teacher attitudes towards language models.

Also referring to the situation in Europe, Karlfried Knapp says:

> I can only speak for the situation in Germany here, which is deplorable. Apart from adopting more communicative approaches to teaching (as a consequence of the pragmatic turn in the 1970s), a greater tolerance for errors (as a consequence of early sequence-oriented SLA research in the 1980s) and a more recent acknowledgement of linguistic diversity in the foreign language classroom (with little practical consequences), recent developments in AL so far have had an impact on language education in Germany only here and there. One main reason for this is the fact that language teachers in Germany are educated as philologists in the first place, with a strong emphasis on literature in their courses of study, and that acquiring background knowledge relevant for the practical task of teaching languages, such as knowledge from AL, occupies only a rather small part of their training.

This supports Johannes Wagner's point mentioned above.

## 10.5 Some impact

AL research has done better in some contexts (subdomains of AL and geographical domains) than others, according to Patricia Duff:

> Educational practice is influenced by much more than theory and research, e.g. by parental or participant demand, by language education policies, institutional constraints, etc. I think there are more options now for learning and for accessing different tools independently, e.g., via the internet, distance learning, etc., than ever before. Immersion (one way and two-way), CLIL, corpus-based/data-driven, usage-based and multimodal approaches have definitely improved because of AL research.

Nina Spada concludes that:

> AL has had an influence/impact on some aspects of language education but it is difficult to measure the extent to which it has had any direct improvements on language education, particularly when "improvement" is measured in terms of language outcomes in relation to amount of classroom instruction. In my opinion, a number of areas within AL have impacted on language education, and this is mainly due to the fact that applied linguists do often adopt an interdisciplinary approach. Learning theory and cognitivism have informed and guided teaching and classroom practice towards more process orientation and learner-centeredness, or

rather learning-centeredness. SLA and FLA research has led to more task and project-oriented approaches and methodologies as well as a rethinking of aims and competencies to be fostered in language learning.

For William Grabe, the most important positive effect is in the move toward ethical use of tests as a major contribution to teaching: "So much depends on tests, citizenship, grants, jobs. Test developers need to be aware of the uses and misuses their tests can be used for." Elana Shohamy refers to "tests as power-tools and tests as policy, with tests driving the curriculum. With that, ethical aspects of testing became important." William Grabe:

> Studies like those conducted by Norris and Ortega (2000) may tell us something about the advantages of form-focused instruction, but how does that reach the classroom? And then there are many types of class-rooms; first world classrooms, third world classrooms, bilingual ones, monolingual ones, how does that basic research relate to all those different classrooms?

Kathleen Bailey sees the work of Labov and other sociolinguists, that has led to a better understanding of language varieties and a rejection (at least among applied linguists) of the notion of standard and non-standard varieties, as a positive effect on teaching and learning.

The growing awareness that there is not one perfect language teaching method based on research on learning styles, strategy use and other individual differences may be one of the most significant contributions, but it is also something that "the larger public" will not completely appreciate or accept, since there will continue to be claims that such and such is the perfect way to learn a language in three weeks. With good marketing and pseudo research it will attract attention, and the disillusion it generates will rarely become public. Research showing that such magical methods do not exist is less likely to hit the headlines of popular magazines.

Related to this is the renewed interest that Peter Robinson sees in aptitude treatment interaction:

> There is an increasing sense of the importance of individual differences in areas such as motivation and aptitude, and of the need to accommodate them instructionally, and this is perhaps the most important contribution work in AL can make to education, I feel, and it is a growing area.

Linked to this are the moderately positive impressions Jean-Marc Dewaele has:

> Nothing massive, because there are no miraculous solutions. But the work on motivation and group dynamics has led to reflection on how to create a positive foreign language environment. Also, the importance of authentic use of the FL has strengthened the case for Erasmus exchanges

and study abroad. The work on lingua franca and multicompetence has hopefully contributed to making language users and FL teachers less guilty (and obsessed) about not sounding like native speakers.

Chuming Wang is careful in his assessment of the contribution of research to education practices:

> In general, findings from AL research have contributed to our understanding of the L2 learning process and those factors relating to language teaching. And this understanding can inform L2 teaching practice to some extent. For example, the interaction-based research has deepened our understanding of the L2 learning process and findings in this area have improved classroom instruction.

Jim Lantolf and Norbert Schmitt feel that the impact of AL on teaching should go through teacher education and they are not too positive about this. In their view, too much time is spent on fluency and pedagogy rather than on the development of a deep insight into the target language. Most of the informants agree that major changes through newly educated and beginning teachers are unlikely: they first have to survive in classes and are typically "domesticated" by their colleagues, who see no reason to change. Referring to the situation in Spain, María del Pilar García Mayo mentions that there are relevant research findings on interaction and task-based approaches, but they have little impact because teachers are not aware of them. She sees it as the applied linguists' task to fill the gap between research and teaching by reaching out to the teacher community. She also sees possibilities for generativist linguistics to contribute to educational issues, as recent research on this topic has shown.

Howard Nicholas sees a positive development in this respect: "There is also an acknowledgement that the practice in teaching is not just a matter of implementing research findings, because the teaching profession has its own complexities that need to be engaged with." Carmen Munoz is careful in her assessment of the impact of communicative language teaching:

> To a certain extent, communicative language teaching principles have been adopted in syllabi of educational systems in many countries, though this has not always led to an improvement of language education. Task-based language teaching, though still with limited implementation, seems promising, as seems aptitude treatment interaction.

The impact on teaching takes place through textbooks, according to Norbert Schmitt. Most teachers faithfully follow the textbook and there could be a washback effect by improving the textbooks on the basis of research findings. Still, even then William Grabe's point remains: how is that renewed textbook used in different types of classrooms?

New insights based on corpus research have provided us with a new perspective on language, in which not grammar, but fixed expressions, are the core of the curriculum. Diane Larsen-Freeman is, however, not convinced: "How do you set up a syllabus around fixed expressions and corpus data? There is no inherent order."

Few informants refer to communicative language learning as a contribution of research to teaching. Zoltán Dörnyei says:

> Perhaps the communicative approach is an improvement, but I am not sure. It seems to me that the various teaching infrastructures in the world are so rigid, conservative and inherently flawed that it is virtually impossible to improve them as a whole. Instead, we can provide the small minority of motivated and dynamic teachers with ammunition.

Some informants see awareness raising as a direct application of research into teaching. Suresh Canagarajah propagates a radical reform of language teaching, in which students are made aware of the use of multiple languages and where they learn to "shuttle between languages and not adhere to prescribed norms". Through the discovery of that shuttling between languages and varieties the language learning takes place.

Referring to second and foreign language education in western Europe, Jan Hulstijn sees the development of the CEFR as having impact on education. But, as mentioned in Chapter 6, in various papers he has voiced his concerns about the CEFR, echoing critical views on it by others.

Along with various other informants, Margaret Thomas notices a change of attitude toward errors: "A positive development is the growth of communicative language teaching that trusts learners to put together sentences and not be afraid to make errors." Rebecca Oxford sees an "on-going, global interest in language learning strategies and strategy instruction, despite theoretical contention about strategies among some researchers in the AL field". Research is always secondary to politics at different levels, according to Mike Long:

> In general, state and federal politicians and corporate interests overwhelm any serious impact research findings could and should have, as witness the dire situation in Arizona, the virtual disappearance of genuine bilingual and immersion K-12 programs throughout the country, the shrinkage in numbers of students at all levels studying foreign languages, and the continued housing (burial?) of most university language programs in literature departments, where foreign languages are "taught" (I use the term loosely) by faculty, part-time lecturers and teaching assistants whose interests lie in literature and many of whom have little knowledge about, and less interest in, language teaching, let alone SLA or AL.

The impact of research also depends on the quality of that research, says Keith Johnson:

I constantly find students (and others!) who do "bad"/mediocre research and seek to apply findings as "facts" to teaching situations. Belief in the value of research has reached silly proportions, and wisdom is often replaced by quantities of meaningless information. This is not to say, though, that a research-based approach to teaching is not a worthy or a possible aim. But we have to be more critical about our research, and how we apply its findings, by giving due consideration to the huge number of variables that affect the teaching process, and how we gauge success therein. Direct application of small-scale research to educational issues is often facile.

Durk Gorter expresses similar views: "There is little influence because most work is far removed from daily classroom practice and there is too little well controlled implementation of new ideas." Keiko Koda does not feel that the gap between classroom and research is problematic. Her views are clear: "Research should inform teaching. If we do classroom based research we don't really contribute to theory."

Rosamond Mitchell sees some positive signs:

AL has supported the democratization/massification of language education, providing rationales and justifications for more varied pedagogic approaches, in particular for more meaning-based approaches (task based learning). AL has assisted the development and evaluation of these newer approaches to pedagogy, even if the impulse driving them came from wider social forces (e.g. the CLIL movement). AL has also provided technical tools enabling the alignment of language education with output-driven educational philosophies.

According to Hannele Dufva there should be more attention to the link between theory and praxis. This can be done by bringing researchers and teachers together:

In my local community, we have aimed at strengthening the collaboration between researchers, teacher educators, teachers, students and policy-makers by creating a "consortium" (kielikampus.jyu.fi) – one of the aims of which is to increase our societal impact in the area of language education.

Rebecca Oxford is also of the view that such cooperation between researchers and teachers has impact: "I have seen a few research partnerships between university researchers and public school teachers, and in those partnerships a great deal of sharing occurs."

## 10.6 Substantial to huge impact

Paul Nation thinks:

The effect has been enormous. I attribute the effect to the amount of publications about AL and the ever-increasing number of research-based diplomas and masters' degrees in AL. These two sources of information have made language teachers, especially teachers of English, much better informed so that classroom practice is generally more rational and effective.

Joseph Lo Bianco is equally positive: "A huge difference, basing pedagogy on a richer set of factors, improvement in design of programs, and classroom interaction, much improved knowledge of links between in-school and out-of-school realities. Much more, too."

According to Lourdes Ortega, the research on immersion has led to the development of similar programs all over the world, in particular the development of Content and Language Integrated Learning (CLIL) in Europe. David Singleton also sees this as an important development, but the effects he has seen are not extensive. Fred Genesee remarks that "the new frontier is the pedagogy of immersion". In his view, immersion and CLIL have proven to be affected by substantial research. With research instruments like observation protocols and CA analyses of classroom interactions, AL research could certainly play a significant role.

Alan Juffs is also largely positive:

I think that the influence has been significant. When I started as a language teacher, Krashen's influence was very strong. The research in AL has brought back the need to focus on form (rather than forms), and resulted in communicative language teaching paying more attention to bottom-up processing as well as top-down schema development.

Few informants are as positive as Ruiying Yang, who bases herself on her experiences in China:

I think AL has led to a very big improvement of language education. The studies of language system from a pedagogic perspective, the insights into L2 learning process and the methods to facilitate learning and acquisition, etc. have changed classroom instruction dramatically. Teachers and instructors equipped with AL knowledge can make informed decisions and carry out their teaching activities more effectively and creatively. 30 years ago, in the English language teaching class in China, the most frequent activities for learners were to listen to the teachers, and to repeat and memorize limited forms. Now in a L2 classroom, learners may carry out problem-solving and critical thinking tasks, doing evaluations and giving presentations. They learn to articulate their ideas and to communicate meaningfully. I think such changes have been brought along by the development of AL as well as teacher education.

Anne Burns argues that the enhanced awareness of the sociocultural context of learning can be seen as a real improvement:

Numerous studies have now shown us the importance of the socio-cultural, as well as the cognitive and affective dimensions of the classroom. I believe this has also led to richer accounts of the opportunities and affordances (to use van Lier's term) that are mediated by the nature of interaction between students and teachers.

Many informants appear to be struggling with Stephen Krashen's relevance and legacy. Patsy Lightbown says:

> Thus, I would have to say, for example, that Krashen had an enormous impact on my area of focus, even if that impact was largely in the creation of a huge straw target for researchers to joust against. And for those academics who believe that the straw target has been toppled, it would be important to read professional development material written for teachers. His hypothesis that comprehensible input is essentially all that is needed for successful acquisition remains influential.

Several informants, including Tim McNamara, feel that Krashen's claims are not supported by adequate research. Celeste Kinginger, as referred to earlier, sees a negative impact of Krashen's ideas on language teaching. Still, many informants see him as a leader and a number of them argue that some of his ideas, in particular with respect to implicit and explicit learning, are supported by neurolinguistic research.

## 10.7 Conclusion

There seems to be a majority among the informants that feels that research has, at least for some aspects, had an impact. The claims we sometimes make about the relevance of research for teaching may be overstated. This may have to do with the growing gap between researchers as practitioners and with the inherent trend to conservatism in the teaching profession. Some informants feel that the lack of impact is to be blamed on the teacher educators who do not manage to foreground research and findings in their programs. But the distance many researchers have to practice from makes such views somewhat moot. Saying how teachers should teach is easy, managing a class of more or less motivated adolescents learning French is not. Robert Phillipson phrases this somewhat more strongly:

> One of my convictions is that while I have remained a teacher of English throughout 50 years of professional life, combining the improvement of my students' English while working with them on applied linguistic topics or sociolinguistic issues of many kinds, the UK/US "experts" generally gave up actual teaching English several decades ago. They pontificate from a theoretical pedestal that is often detached from classroom realities, theorizing ESL, and occasionally doing empiricist studies.

Second language teaching seems to be more open to innovation based on research than foreign language teaching, and that is the case on both sides of the Atlantic. However, China seems to be a wonderful exception.

There is not enough research to actually evaluate new trends in language teaching, apart from immersion and CLIL. Also, the concepts and labels used are not always clearly defined.

Developments on language testing have an indirect effect on language teaching and through positive backwash this is seen as a positive influence. For some, the development of the CEFR (Common European Framework of Reference) is a positive factor, but that view is also contested. Anna Mauranen observes that:

> in more specific domains, a greater AL influence can be discerned: in the teaching of writing, developments in text and discourse analysis have directed teaching to more text-based approaches away from the sentence, and corpus linguistics has affected the perception of the target language. Genre analysis has changed EAP teaching considerably.

Andrea Tyler also mentions the growth of research on writing as a process as a major trend.

# 11 Concluding remarks

This project started out with the title: *A Sociology of Applied Linguistics*. Then it became *A Social History of Applied Linguistics 1980–2010*, then *A Recent History of Applied Linguistics*, and finally it ended up as *A History of Applied Linguistics: From 1980 to the present*. Having come to the end of the thinking and writing process, I realize that maybe this book is not even that. It is not a history in which the development over time of ideas is followed or in which the main controversies are put in their historic context. Nor is it a description of how the main figures in the field formed and changed their views and how that relates to changes in the larger societal context. Nor is it an analysis of how leading research groups or institutions and the people associated with it developed with details on the internal politics, who worked with whom, who hated who and why. It is none of that. What remains is essentially the state of play of a field; a screenshot of what may or may not be a community or a discipline.

I have come to this view based on the responses to five questions that I asked to discover how a selected group of applied linguists defined the field and its developments. The first question was how the field is defined. It turns out that there are three perspectives: one that sees AL as a discipline aiming at solving real world problems with linguistic means and tools, the second that equates AL with SLD, and a third that sees AL as including everything about language, apart from formal linguistic description. My informants were spread over these groups, but there seemed to be a majority that favored the pragmatic, open definition of the third group.

The second question was who are the leaders in AL. The rankings show that there is consensus on who are the top leaders. These leaders have academic weight, are active in the field and support the development of young talent. In a sense, they define the field by their work and presence. They act as role models for younger researchers. There seems to be some convergence in the names mentioned, though a significant portion of the informants do not see AL as a coherent and uniform field but rather as a set of subfields that each have their own leaders.

Who are the prototypical applied linguists? It could be argued that our top ten leaders qualify. What they have in common is that they publish in the same journals, write books for the same publishers, and present at the same conferences, that they have academic status and a good publication record, that they have changed positions both geographically and content-wise, that they are active in professional organizations and act as editors of books and journals and that they are well connected. They do not neces-sarily work in the same area and on the same topics, but they have their favorite topics: James Lantolf and Merrill Swain for Social Cultural Theory (SCT), Diane Larsen-Freeman for complexity theory, Henry Widdowson for discourse, and Claire Kramsch for cultural and ecological approaches to foreign language learning. Though there are clearly differences in view and theoretical orientation, in general they respect each other's work. It seems that the leaders, probably combined with the publishers, are what binds the field, more than research topics, definitions of the field, impact on language teaching or views on what constitutes the core of the AL literature. A majority of the leaders do work that relates to language teaching, though the distance from what really goes on in classrooms is fairly large for most of them.

The third source is the information given about articles and books. As pointed out earlier, the list of articles and books mentioned is very long and there are just a handful of publications that are generally seen as core for the field. There are many publications from outside the field, which supports the view that AL is conceptually interdisciplinary in the sense that ideas, theories and research methods from other disciplines are imported. The multitude of publications mentioned is, on the one hand, a sign that there is basically no content that is shared by all applied linguists; on the other hand, it shows the ability of the field to react creatively to developments in other areas and apply them in its research.

There does not seem to be a common core of publications that define the field. Whether this is a specific problem for AL, I do not know. A similar survey to the one reported on here among psychologists or cultural anthro-pologists is likely to show an equally disparate pattern. It may be a natural tendency of disciplines to fractionize and reassemble parts of the old dis-cipline into new coalitions. This may not be a reason to despair about the future of AL and, indeed, we have seen the emergence of sub-communities, working on testing, SLA, English as a Lingua Franca (ELF), SCT and so on. There seems to be little ground for any of these subdisciplines to claim that they are the "real" AL, even for those that in the early days of the field were defined as the core constituents.

The fourth question concerned the trends the informants have witnessed over the last decades. There is a wide range of topics the informants refer to. The field has moved in many ways and directions, but there are probably two main issues to be noted. The first is the decline of the impact of formal linguistics as a major theoretical basis for AL. The other major trend is the move away from an emphasis on psycholinguistic mechanisms in individual language users and learners to cognition as socially embedded. The "social turn" was, or maybe still is, a reaction to the impact of psycholinguistics and its focus on controlled, experimental, statistically based research in the field. For the credibility of the field the "hard science" approach in psycholinguistics is seen as important, but many informants feel that it is no longer needed, since AL has a well-established position in many universities all over the world.

The fifth question was how informants see the relationship between research and teaching. Again, there was a range of views. For some informants even having this item in the questionnaire was too much of a sign that AL is basically, or only, on learning and using additional languages. But the majority agrees that many of the "real world problems" AL can contribute to are related to language learning and instruction. Views are divided over the contribution of research to the improvement of language teaching. Some informants see a negative impact, others see no impact at all, but for the majority the impact has been substantial. What it contributed is a move from behaviorist approaches to language learning to more communicatively oriented approaches. Part of that is related to language policy and political and social developments outside the field. The impact on better teaching methods has been limited, but the now generally accepted notion that there is no optimal, one-size-fits-all approach to language learning is an important contribution. Individuals differ in many respects and so does their learning.

Do these sources of information converge? The global picture that emerges is one of what might be labeled as a "community of practice". There is a feeling of shared interests and goals and the intention to improve these through learning from others. But maybe the seventeenth-century term "invisible college" is more appropriate here. Robert Merton, the founding father of the sociology of science, presents the following definition:

> Invisible colleges can be construed sociologically as clusters of geographically dispersed scientists who engage in more frequent cognitive interaction with one another than they do with others in the larger community of science. At the outset, the members of an emerging invisible college regard themselves as major reference individuals and regard themselves collectively as a reference group, whose opinions of their work matter deeply and whose standards of cognitive performance are taken as binding.
>
> (1977: 6)

Of course, geographical dispersion has become less of an issue in the twenty-first century than it was in the seventeenth century, but the picture of more interaction within the group than outside the group without closing off such external contacts is typical of AL. In that sense, a discipline is defined more by what a group of people do than by the verbal labels they use to describe it.

It may be enough to feel that we belong to that community more than any other community in the academic world. Within that community there may be more narrowly scoped communities of practice, like the testing community or people working on second language writing, but belonging to that niche community does not exclude the possibility of feeling engaged at a higher level, too.

In Chapter 9, data on AL and citations of publications are presented. This information is somewhat different in nature from that in other chapters, since it is not based on informants' views but on their publications as they are cited (or not). The data show that citations and impact factors are relevant now, much more so than in the 1980s and early 1990s. The analyses presented tell us little about the structure of the field of AL, who cites who, and who is co-cited with whom, but more advanced analytical tools are emerging that will provide that kind of information. A comparison of who are seen as leaders and their impact shows that leadership depends on academic status as measured with citation indices, but only partly. Other characteristics of leaders, such as stimulating and supporting young colleagues, contribution to the field through organizations and publishers, are also important. The data also show that AL follows developments in the social sciences closely in this respect, making it move away even further from the literature community where this type of citation analysis is still problematic, both technically and in terms of attitudes.

Chapter 8 presents some research applications of CDST. It is argued that CDST is effectively a paradigm shift, with all that entails. Many of the assumptions about research in the area of AL as defined in this book, appear to be problematic if one takes a CDST perspective. For some of the new ideas, we do not even have the right words, which makes it hard to present them. There is one area of AL where CDST is striving: research on attitudes and motivation in language learning. This shows that for a fundamental shift in perspective it is necessary that some of the leading researchers in a field take on the new ideas and propagate them widely. At least for this area of research the Dynamic Turn has already taken place. More areas are likely to follow, but there is still substantial resistance that needs to be overcome.

When I started this project, I was convinced that AL as a discipline existed and that what I did was at the core of that enterprise. The conferences and workshops I attended were all in line with what I was working on, and I published in the same journals and books as my colleagues and friends. We met at the same places and shared our likes and dislikes. Sometimes the input from other disciplines would play a role, but that would ultimately be integrated with what we already did. As mentioned in the first chapter, my perception of the field was defined by my social setting and so were my preferences. I realized that I was the product of the system I was part of. My views on generative grammar were not based on a deep and thorough insight in the theory, but the result of interactions with people in my universities and the Max Planck Institute in Nijmegen. I was socialized in that setting and conformed to the norms there. Not that I just followed the fashions, I went my own way and explored new avenues beyond the confines of my upbringing. But I always felt that I was a real applied linguist. I had a vague notion that there were other people that held other views, and that the conception of AL was not as straightforward as I felt it to be, but I never worried about it.

The work with bilingual schools in the Netherlands clearly was AL, in the sense that it contributed to solving real world problems. It brought me into real classes where pupils became individuals rather than types of informants. It was also a good example of the right kind of problem finding and solving: it was not me who wanted to develop a quality control system for bilingual schools, but the schools themselves.

Our work on language attrition might also be seen as another "real" AL activity, but here the problem to be solved did come from the research and language policy community and not so much from those exhibiting or suffering from language attrition. The same is true for the work on relearning of forgotten languages. Though I would still claim that this contributes to solving real world problems, the initiative to work on this came from inside the ivory tower.

But I ask myself, why was I not interested in discourse analysis and conversational analysis at the time? From time to time I would attend presentations in which five seconds of speech were analyzed exhaustively, preferably without taking into account the conversational context, with unfounded assumptions about the speaker's intentions and the significance of minor details. The research community I was part of at the time was the Interfaculty Unit for Language and Speech, which connected research at the Max Planck Institute for Psycholinguistics and the Faculty of Arts of the University of Nijmegen. The researchers at the MPI, both residents and those visiting, were a constant source of inspiration, and of course they all held on to the experimental empirical approach. Introspection, and more generally qualitative data, were looked at with suspicion and doubts about the ecological validity of single word recognition tasks were seen as irrelevant. A typical reaction to the more qualitative approach that began to start in the 1980s was Wolfgang Klein's review of the Faerch and Kaspar book on introspection in SLA from 1989. The title of his review was "Introspection into what?" and that summarized the MPI perspective neatly.

For a while I became interested in SCT, in part because I liked the people who were working on it. Though it has brilliant thinking behind it, in the end it became too nebulous for me and required too much adherence to the scriptures. Also the emphasis on instruction ran counter to my own intuitions based on my experiences and research on bilingual schools and CLIL. My observations, underpinned by substantial evaluative research, were that pupils in CLIL classrooms acquired high levels of proficiency in English both in perception and in production, mainly through using it rather than learning the rules. The pupils' interest in rules followed their acquisition of implicit knowledge, and they wanted the rules to back up their intuitions, more or less along the lines of Krashen's monitor theory.

Now, having come to the end of a journey, what has changed? As I mentioned before, for a long time I considered myself as core AL. Now, I realize that my view was myopic and narrow and that I have missed, or at any rate not seen, important developments. Maybe that is not something to worry about. Trying to keep up with all developments in AL and connected areas is basically impossible, and having a broad knowledge of the field requires both time to read and a good memory, both of which were and will be lacking. But having the overview of the field that this study provided will certainly help me to stay open-minded and sensitive to new developments, both within and outside the field.

In a recent e-mail exchange, William Grabe said the following:

> The process of having everyone consider key resources that shape each person's thinking is still with me. I exchanged lists with Jan Hulstijn and it's interesting how different they were between his and mine. That is because he truly is an SLA person with reading and vocabulary, and now assessment, as the outlets for his organizing idea of "what is L2 proficiency?" My organizing idea is "what is L2 reading ability?", which led me much more outside of SLA. That was clearly reflected in our two lists. It helps me understand better why I am an outlier to some extent.

My reaction was: "My conclusion of the whole process is that we are basically all outsiders, we have a part that overlaps with others, but probably the larger part is different even from people we think are doing the same things as we do."

A final question remains. To what extent does AL exist as a scientific discipline? We have seen that the answer may depend on the definition used. As a research area that looks at various aspects of the learning and teaching of languages, it certainly exists and this connection will be seen by most applied linguists as the most important one. Things are less clear for the psycholinguistic part of SLA. This seems to be running out of steam within the AL community, while more socially oriented approaches to language learning, based on identity, multilingualism and ecological considerations, are likely to grow. As a discipline that seeks to deal with real world problems, AL will continue to look eagerly for individuals and groups suffering from some language or communication related ailment waiting to be asked to provide an answer. As for the infrastructure, AL as a discipline is clearly doing well, despite local struggles with formal linguists. There are numerous MA and PhD programs in various parts of the world, and enrollments are good. There are at least two overarching organizations, AAAL and AILA, which give structure to the field globally. There are a number of AL journals that are doing well. AL has clearly overcome the inferiority syndrome it was suffering from in the past, though taking on the role of a serious research oriented movement will go at the expense of dealing with real world problems.

When invited to take part in this project Aneta Pavlenko reacted enthusiastically and wrote: "It looks like our baby field is finally coming of age." Maybe this book has a role to play in the maturation and self-definition of AL, but given the biases in the selection of informants and the questions asked, it will continue to be "a" or "my" rather than "the" history. Other perspectives and other voices will lead to different outcomes that are equally as valid or invalid as the ones presented in this book.

## References

Klein, W. (1989) "Introspection into what? Review of C. Faerch and G. Kaspar (eds), Introspection in second language research 1987", *Contemporary Psychology, A Journal of Reviews*, vol. 34, no. 12: 1119–20.

Merton, R. (1977) *The Sociology of Science: An Episodic Memoir*, Chicago: Southern Illinois University Press.

# Appendix 1

## The questionnaire

**Questionnaire on the Sociology of Applied Linguistics 1980–2010**

This is part of a study on the Sociology of Applied Linguistics (AL). In this study I want to draw a picture of the development of AL from 1980 until 2010. Major questions are: what were the major trends, what theories emerged and faded, who were the intellectual and organizational leaders in the field, who influenced who and why did the field develop the way it did? For this study I want to interview/get information from a group of people who have been influential in this process. In my view you are one of them. Below you find a list of issues I would like have your reaction to. All information will be treated as strictly confidential.

What is your educational background (BA/MA/PhD, what universities and
  when)?
How did you get involved with Applied Linguistics?
What is your definition of Applied Linguistics?
Who are the most important/influential leaders in the field? Why are they
  important?
Who have you been most influenced by and who did you influence in your
  view?
What are the 5–10 most important articles for you over these 30 years?
What are the 5–10 most important books for you over these 30 years?
What are the major trends you have noticed over these 30 years?
To what extent, and if so how, has AL research led to an improvement of
  language education?

# Appendix 2
## Definitions of AL from AILA and AAAL

### AILA

Applied Linguistics is an interdisciplinary field of research and practice dealing with practical problems of language and communication that can be identified, analysed or solved by applying available theories, methods and results of Linguistics or by developing new theoretical and methodological frameworks in Linguistics to work on these problems. Applied Linguistics differs from Linguistics in general mainly with respect to its explicit orientation towards practical, everyday problems related to language and communication.

The problems Applied Linguistics deals with range from aspects of the linguistic and communicative competence of the individual such as first or second language acquisition, literacy, language disorders, etc. to language and communication related problems in and between societies such as e.g. language variation and linguistic discrimination, multilingualism, language conflict, language policy and language planning.

(source: www.aila.info/en/)

### AAAL

Applied Linguistics itself is an interdisciplinary field of inquiry that addresses a broad range of language-related issues in order to improve the lives of individuals and conditions in society. It draws on a wide range of theoretical, methodological, and educational approaches from various disciplines – from the humanities to the social, cognitive, medical, and natural sciences – as it develops its own knowledge-base about language, its users and uses, and their underlying social and material conditions.

(source: www.AAAL.org)

# Appendix 3
## Index and total number of citations

*Table A.1* Index and total number of citations

| Name | *h*-index | Number of citations of three most cited publications | | | |
|------|-----------|------|------|------|------|
| | | 1 | 2 | 3 | Total |
| Bachman | 36 | 4,977 | 2,829 | 322 | 8,128 |
| Bailey | 31 | 1,467 | 600 | 366 | 2,433 |
| Bardel | 17 | 86 | 25 | 24 | 135 |
| Bardovi-Harlig | 39 | 473 | 403 | 296 | 1,172 |
| Burns | 25 | 862 | 201 | 139 | 1,202 |
| Bygate | 15 | 653 | 497 | 102 | 1,252 |
| Byrnes | 28 | 248 | 185 | 104 | 537 |
| Canagarajah | 33 | 1,337 | 335 | 332 | 2,004 |
| Candlin | 33 | 1,956 | 707 | 428 | 3,091 |
| Cenoz | 30 | 248 | 222 | 213 | 683 |
| Chapelle | 34 | 1,060 | 394 | 316 | 1,770 |
| Cohen | 34 | 2,400 | 595 | 415 | 3,410 |
| Cook | 38 | 1,862 | 1,081 | 881 | 3,824 |
| Crandal | 7 | 165 | 164 | 115 | 444 |
| Crystal | 61 | 9,321 | 5,283 | 4,354 | 18,958 |
| Cumming | 31 | 566 | 188 | 186 | 940 |
| Davies | 28 | 439 | 375 | 284 | 1,098 |
| De Bot | 36 | 676 | 282 | 279 | 1,237 |
| De Houwer | 15 | 517 | 376 | 172 | 1,065 |
| DeKeyser | 27 | 534 | 528 | 366 | 1,428 |
| Dörnyei | 53 | 718 | 1,580 | 1,297 | 3,595 |
| Duff | 31 | 320 | 314 | 281 | 915 |
| Dufva | 13 | 95 | 41 | 38 | 174 |
| Ellis, N. | 54 | 958 | 459 | 384 | 1,801 |
| Ellis, R. | 73 | 9,471 | 5,028 | 2,439 | 16,938 |
| Flynn | 22 | 396 | 392 | 156 | 944 |
| Freeman | 35 | 625 | 472 | 428 | 1,525 |
| Garcia Mayo | 13 | 141 | 82 | 67 | 290 |
| Gass | 53 | 2,138 | 1,255 | 717 | 4,110 |
| Genesee | 54 | 1,179 | 513 | 502 | 2,194 |
| Gorter | 18 | 174 | 161 | 151 | 486 |
| Grabe | 33 | 981 | 904 | 823 | 2,708 |
| Gregg | 16 | 430 | 165 | 120 | 715 |
| Gullberg | 20 | 175 | 81 | 64 | 320 |
| Hawkins | 24 | 633 | 490 | 393 | 1,516 |
| Hulstijn, | 30 | 702 | 520 | 427 | 1,649 |
| Hyltenstam | 29 | 407 | 195 | 168 | 770 |
| Johnson, Karen | 12 | 622 | 549 | 258 | 1,429 |
| Johnson, Keith | 25 | 888 | 480 | 418 | 1,786 |
| Kellerman | 28 | 485 | 383 | 355 | 1,223 |
| Kelly Hall | 20 | 235 | 166 | 159 | 560 |
| Kinginger | 16 | 180 | 168 | 167 | 515 |

*Table A.1* (continued)

| Name | h-index | Number of citations of three most cited publications | | | |
|------|---------|------|------|------|------|
| | | 1 | 2 | 3 | Total |
| Knapp | 17 | 209 | 174 | 161 | 544 |
| Koda | 25 | 478 | 173 | 150 | 801 |
| Kramsch | 48 | 3,276 | 1,801 | 413 | 5,490 |
| Krashen | 62 | 8,710 | 6,755 | 5,931 | 21,396 |
| Lambert | 14 | 197 | 129 | 80 | 406 |
| Lantolf | 38 | 1,265 | 1,003 | 600 | 2,868 |
| Lanza | 12 | 349 | 227 | 44 | 620 |
| Larsen-Freeman | 38 | 2,618 | 2,077 | 575 | 5,270 |
| Laufer | 42 | 705 | 643 | 612 | 1,960 |
| Lightbown | 35 | 3,094 | 614 | 612 | 4,320 |
| Lo Bianco | 15 | 516 | 122 | 113 | 751 |
| Long | 68 | 2,618 | 1,393 | 1,106 | 5,117 |
| McGroarty | 18 | 383 | 119 | 100 | 602 |
| McNamara | 24 | 837 | 272 | 205 | 1,314 |
| Makoni | 18 | 324 | 62 | 60 | 446 |
| Mauranen | 30 | 495 | 330 | 176 | 1,001 |
| Meara | 38 | 309 | 292 | 292 | 893 |
| Mitchell | 18 | 1,342 | 181 | 138 | 1,661 |
| Munoz | 14 | 157 | 51 | 34 | 242 |
| Nation | 45 | 2,701 | 643 | 353 | 3,697 |
| Nicholas | 14 | 349 | 77 | 70 | 496 |
| Ortega | 20 | 1,073 | 384 | 289 | 1,746 |
| Oxford | 65 | 6,269 | 964 | 808 | 8,041 |
| Pavlenko | 42 | 631 | 620 | 309 | 1,560 |
| Pennycook | 45 | 2,073 | 1,206 | 1,061 | 4,340 |
| Pienemann | 24 | 899 | 595 | 518 | 2,012 |
| Rampton | 32 | 1,675 | 504 | 295 | 2,474 |
| Ricento | 15 | 239 | 225 | 223 | 687 |
| Robinson | 34 | 1,268 | 614 | 420 | 2,302 |
| Rüschoff | 13 | 146 | 127 | 37 | 310 |
| Schmidt | 29 | 2,950 | 2,846 | 1,147 | 6,943 |
| Schmitt | 32 | 1,139 | 608 | 607 | 2,354 |
| Schumann | 30 | 1,045 | 695 | 367 | 2,107 |
| Seidlhofer | 31 | 613 | 581 | 275 | 1,469 |
| Sharwood Smith | 26 | 684 | 654 | 365 | 1,703 |
| Shohamy | 34 | 545 | 513 | 229 | 1,287 |
| Shuy | 33 | 364 | 226 | 221 | 811 |
| Singleton | 12 | 608 | 461 | 169 | 1,238 |
| Skutnabb-Kangas | 37 | 1,481 | 900 | 500 | 2,881 |
| Soraci | 36 | 505 | 288 | 273 | 1,066 |
| Spada | 28 | 3,094 | 612 | 542 | 4,248 |
| Spolsky | 38 | 1,199 | 715 | 417 | 2,331 |
| Swain | 65 | 4,977 | 3,659 | 2,304 | 10,940 |
| Tarone | 40 | 579 | 608 | 512 | 1,699 |
| Thomas | 12 | 159 | 99 | 78 | 336 |
| Tucker | 27 | 1,221 | 211 | 188 | 1,620 |
| Tyler | 17 | 400 | 220 | 178 | 798 |
| van Els | 10 | 263 | 92 | 73 | 428 |

*Table A.1* (continued)

| Name | h-index | Number of citations of three most cited publications | | | |
| | | 1 | 2 | 3 | Total |
|---|---|---|---|---|---|
| VanPatten | 35 | 632 | 624 | 622 | 1,878 |
| Wagner | 23 | 1,062 | 217 | 152 | 1,431 |
| Wang | 14 | 158 | 90 | 45 | 293 |
| Weideman | 13 | 49 | 40 | 36 | 125 |
| White | 46 | 1,030 | 776 | 628 | 2,434 |
| Widdowson | 47 | 3,279 | 1,479 | 1,410 | 6,168 |
| Wiley | 15 | 172 | 159 | 143 | 474 |
| Young | 25 | 507 | 190 | 144 | 841 |

# Index

Entries in **bold** denote tables; entries in *italics* denote figures.